Pacifism as Pathology

PACIFISM as PATHOLOGY

Reflections on the Role of
Armed Struggle in North America

Ward Churchill

with Mike Ryan

ARBEITER RING
Winnipeg

Arbeiter Ring Publishing
201E-121 Osborne Street
Winnipeg, Manitoba
Canada R3L 1Y4
phone: 204.942.7058
fax: 204.944.9198
info@arbeiterring.com
www.arbeiterring.com

Printed in Canada by the workers at Hignell Printing

5th printing, 2005

Canadian Cataloguing in Publication Data:

Churchill, Ward.

    Pacifism as pathology

    Includes bibliographical references and index.
    ISBN 1-894037-07-3

1. Peace movements.   2. Pacifism.   3. War—North America
I. Ryan, Mike, 1957–   II. Title.

JZ5538.C48   1998   327.1'72   C98-920110-4

Contents

Diana Oughton, a member of the Weather Underground Organization was killed, along with WUO members Ted Gold and Terry Robbins, on March 6, 1970. They died when bombs they were preparing in the basement of a Greenwich Village townhouse accidentally detonated, thus aborting what might have become the first substantial armed campaign against the state mounted by Euroamerican revolutionaries in the twentieth century. The poem, "For Diana Oughton" appeared in the Berkeley *Tribe*, July 31 of the same year.

FOR DIANA OUGHTON

Sometimes
There is only bullets and hate
      self-sacrifice
               dismembered bodies
and blood –

And all I can see are
the lines of
      cruelty on
our faces.

But when I think of you,
Sister,
      and remember how you
loved the people
      and
fought the struggle
I know what you would say now –

"you don't cry for me
but for yourselves –
That's bullshit!
Why do you only talk of dying for
      Revolution?
Live for it!"

                          – Anonymous

Preface

Power grows from the barrel of a gun.
　　　　　　　　　　　　 – Chairman Mao Tsetung

O kay kids, here we go, my first ever preface to well, an essay. It displays a kind of logic and research methodology that I myself am not capable of emulating while examining the question of political violence, or, more accurately, the efficacy of adopting a political strategy of *non*violence (pacifism). Pacifism is an important issue for anyone interested in the role of violence in political struggle (a subject one can scarcely ignore in today's world). In my opinion, Ward Churchill has done a good job of addressing the subject. By way of an introduction, then, I will add only a few of my own perspectives. Here goes.

The headline of today's *Seattle Times* screamed, "Experts Warn of Food Crisis Ahead." The story, with graphs showing growing population levels, the limitations of the increasingly depleted soil, and lists of experts and pictures, has probably been long forgotten by most of Seattle's residents. The effects were, after all, presented mostly as being visited upon others, elsewhere, the sort of consequence of empire experienced mostly by Third World populations and other equally unimportant groups.

I too tend to get pretty mellow about how events are unfolding on the stage of today's world. As a rule, I pay more attention to what is going on here at home, or my attention is focused in the direction the ruling class media pushes me. Like most Americans, I am affected by or in some way understand that there are those who do not, because of their race and nationality, enjoy the many luxuries available to those of us here in the heartland. Twenty years ago, when I was part of Seattle's Prairie Fire Organizing Committee, we had a term for those who felt it was necessary and appropriate for people out there in the colonies to fight and die in the struggle against international imperialism while intellectually exempting themselves from incurring the same risks and obligations. The expression used by PFOC back in those days was "American exceptionalism."

I think we can agree that the exploited are everywhere and that they are angry. The question of violence and our own direct experience of it is something we will not be able to avoid when the righteous rage of the oppressed manifests itself in increasingly focused and violent forms. When this time comes, it is likely that white pacifists will be the ruling class' first line of defence. If there is any substance at all to this notion, then we might just as well start the process of having this discussion now instead of later, and that is another reason why I am writing this introduction.

In my opinion, peaceful tactics comprise the only form of political agenda that can be sustained during this particular historical period. Armed actions would not further the struggle for justice at present, but they could plainly hurt it (my reference here is to offensive activities rather than to armed self-defense, which is an altogether different matter, in my view). I suspect that when the situation changes everyone will know it, and the time clearly ain't now.

Anyway, Ward and I reached our respective conclusions about pacifism from different directions. His background is academic, as reflected in the title of his essay, "Pacifism As Pathology: Notes on an American Pseudopraxis." In contrast, I just finished an eighteen-year stretch in prison for having been a part of a political organization that bombed, among other places, the headquarters of the Department of Corrections in Olympia; the Bureau of Indian Affairs building in Everett, and the FBI office in the Tacoma federal courthouse.

I have talked about violence in connection with political struggle for a long time and I've engaged in it. I see myself as one who incorrectly applied the tool of revolutionary violence during a period when its use was not appropriate. In doing so, my associates and I paid a terrible price. That cost included the loss of comrades Bruce

Siedel and Ralph Ford (Poe). Poe died while planting a pipe bomb in the refrigeration mechanisms located in the back wall of the Safeway store on 15th, and Bruce was killed in a shootout with police at a failed George Jackson Brigade bank robbery. The cost also included the loss to Seattle's progressive movement of many committed militants, who ended up spending many years in various state and federal prisons.

I served nearly two decades behind bars as a result of armed actions conducted by the George Jackson Brigade. During those years, I studied and restudied the mechanics and applicability of both violence and noviolence to political struggle. I've had plenty of time to learn how to step back and take a look at the larger picture. And, however badly I may represent that picture today, I still find one conclusion inescapable: Pacifism as a strategy of achieving social, political and economic change can only lead to the dead end of liberalism.

Those who denounce the use of political violence as a matter of principle, who advocate nonviolence as a strategy for progress, are wrong. Nonviolence is a tactical question, not a strategic one. The most vicious and violent ruling class in the history of humankind will not give up without a physical fight. Nonviolence as a strategy thus amounts to a form of liberal accommodation and is bound to fail. The question is not *whether* to use violence in the global class struggle to end the rule of international imperialism, but only *when* to use it.

By writing in a way that is supportive of the use of

revolutionary violence, I want to make it clear that I am not talking about self-destructive avenues like political adventurism. Instead, I am merely objecting to the privileges that pacifists are often able to enjoy at the expense of the global class struggle (one does not see too many pacifists of colour these days).

I am not proud of my prison background. At best, I can say that I came out of the prison experience with a bit less damage than many of my peers. But, still, I came out damaged. I don't know how long, if ever, it will take me to really know the depths of that damage. Nonetheless, I managed to do my time in a manner I believe was consistent with communist principles. While I was never the tough guy on the block, and on occasion was seen as a nigger-lovin' commie-fag, I still managed to get by without having to ever snitch on another prisoner or check into protective custody for my own safety. To that extent, I came out okay. But, on the level of having any answers (beyond my limited prison activist's scope), I do not score nearly so well.

With that caveat in mind, what I have to say, and I thank Ward for giving me the opportunity to say it, is this: 99.9 percent of the practitioners of political violence will one day be confronted with imprisonment or death, neither of which is a fun experience. If at some future point we are bound to engage in violent struggle against the government (Gee, why would anyone do that?) it is imperative that we do so in a manner calculated to win. The object *is* to win.

This is what we thought when the class war was being fought and won around the globe, when somewhere between a half-million and a million Americans marched on Washington in 1969, causing H.R. Haldeman to ask President Richard M. Nixon whether this radical event might turn out to be the prelude to a figurative storming of the Winter Palace here in the USA. The television screens of the era, after all, also showed U.S. troops reeling in defeat before Vietnamese liberation forces supplied by both China and the USSR. The same images would shortly be aired with respect to Cambodia and Laos. There were other revolutionary victories in places like Cuba, Nicaragua, Mozambique, and Angola. Substantial guerrilla struggles were being waged at the time in Uruguay, El Salvador, Guatemala, Palestine, Rhodesia, South Africa, the Philippines and elsewhere. We future Brigade members could see a world in which progressive forces were on the offensive internationally and imperialism was everywhere in retreat.

All we needed to do to bring about final victory, it seemed, was apply pressure on the cracks of empire by opening up fronts in the belly of the beast itself. Thus, some of us on the West Coast began to engage in armed struggle in Los Angeles, San Francisco, Sacramento, Portland, Oregon, and Seattle. In certain of these places, notably San Francisco, Seattle and L.A., several groups were doing this work at the same time, and similar units were emerging in major cities across the United States, from Denver to Chicago, from New York to Portland, Maine.

We could readily envision a day when all of these seem-ingly isolated elements would join into one huge fist, battering the whole structure of capitalist oppression to its knees. That was the atmosphere in which the Brigade developed. Conditions seemed genuinely ripe for revo-lution.

We are nowhere near that situation today, and it must be said that the Brigade was even then premature in initiating armed struggle. We made a grave error, one that was costly in terms of human life and suffering. There is nothing wrong with sacrificing today for a tomorrow that is significantly freer from oppression, but, in our case, the sacrifice did not accomplish the desired politi-cal goals. That, I think, was our principle error. How-ever, in spite of all that, as bad as it was, I still tend to feel pride in the fact that we erred on the side of making revolution. If an error is to be made, it seems to me that that's the manner in which it ought to be made.

So, with all of that water under the bridge, you are now presented with the treat of reading Ward's essay on pacifism. I think you will find that his treatment of the subject is well-reasoned and rational. If you disagree, well, that's your right. But, for myself, I enjoyed the reading. It gave me a solid basis for discussing this topic more intelligently, and that, whatever else might be said, is something all of us need rather urgently at the present time.

– Ed Mead

Introduction

"Pacifism as Pathology" Revisited:
Excavating a Debate

The fire this *time* . . .
                                    – Eldridge Cleaver, 1971

t is with considerable pleasure, and a certain degree
of trepidation, that I (re)introduce my essay, "Pacifism as Pathology: Notes on an American
Psuedopraxis," first published more than a decade ago.
My pleasure derives from the extent to which the piece
stimulated what I believe to have been healthy and constructive debate after its initial release in early 1986, a
process which seems even more appropriate at this time.
The trepidation, of course, stems from the fact that, as is
probably true for the author of anything "controversial,"

I was subjected to a significant amount of *ad homonym* attack for displaying the audacity to commit to paper what quite a lot of people were already feeling. One must, however, accept the bad (or idiotic) as well as good (and intelligent) in such matters.

It has been suggested that I provide a bit of information concerning the origins of the essay. Perhaps obviously, it emerged from the matrix of cumulative frustration attending my own ongoing years of activist experience, but there are those who have suspected (correctly) that there was something more specific involved in motivating me to write it. The incident occurred when I accepted an invitation extended by Bob Sipe, an organizer/member of the Midwest Radical Therapy Association, to deliver a workshop at the group's 1981 annual conference, held near Boone, Iowa.

The premise underlying my session was that many people on the left demonstrated an irrational aversion to firearms based upon an abject ignorance of – and consequent intimidation by – the technology itself. Worse, they were intent on glossing over this experiential/skills deficiency by proclaiming such weakness to be both a "moral virtue" and a political dynamic. To my mind, and Sipe's, this translated into a posture of deliberate self-disempowerment on the part of oppositionists, the only possible result of which would be a virtual monopoly of firepower by the very institutional/ideological status quo we radicals were supposedly committed to abolishing. To call such practice self-defeating is to dramatically understate the case.

It was our feeling that an antidote to what we perceived as a psychological log jam might be found in pro-
viding literal "hands on" exposure to weapons for those
who'd never had an opportunity to experience it. Our
thesis was simple enough: only by becoming familiar with
weapons – to some extent "demystifying" them – could
one strip away the kind of psychic baggage which pre-
cluded rational decision-making with respect to their
potential utility. Embrace or repudiation of the use of
weapons was perhaps a personal choice, we maintained,
but in either event the choice needed to be an informed
one ("knowledge is power," eh?).

In the event, the workshop I provided – entitled
"Demystification of the Assault Rifle" – was well attended, in no small part by a group of lesbian feminists
who showed up, as they later acknowledged, mainly to
denounce the whole thing as an exercise in "macho swag-
gering." After two hours of handling a pair of Heckler &
Koch assaut rifles – such "exotic" weapons were used as
expedient to heightening the extent to which demystification occured – learning how and why they were put
together as they were, Q&A on the applicability of various types of guns to different situations, and an altogether
calm discussion of the role of arms in assorted political
contexts, they'd changed their minds in some significant
respects. "I still have some very large questions in my
mind concerning the appropriateness of armed struggle,
and doubt that I'd ever participate in it," said one woman,

"but I have to admit that this has changed my outlook on guns and at least some of the people who use them. It's going to cause me to look at a lot of things – the Black Panthers, for example – in a whole new way. So, and I'm really surprised to find myself saying this, I think the workshop was really worthwhile and that we should have more of them in the future. In fact, the instructor offered to come back next year and teach people how to actually shoot these things, and I think I'm going to take him up on it."[1]

One would think that, given this sort of favourable response – and it is indicative – similar exercises in demystification/personal empowerment might have been encouraged by the Association. Instead, I'd barely left the conference grounds en route back to Colorado before Claude Steiner, a senior organizer, demanded an "emergency plenary meeting." When it was convened that evening, he advanced a resolution for ratification by the membership prohibiting such workshops from ever again being conducted under the organization's auspices, and barring anyone from bringing a firearm (or simulated firearm) to a conference for any purpose.[2] The measure passed by a decisive margin, although it was observed that no one who had actually attended the session, including several devout pacifists, voted in favour of such restrictions.

As if this weren't bad enough, a question was then posed by an opponent as to whether, should the cops at some point show up at at conference, those who had voted in favour of the resolution would be prepared to either disarm them or physically eject them. An amendment was then quickly put forth and ratified whcih exempted "police and other civil authorities" from the otherwise blanket ban on weapons. For at least some people, this finally said it all, validating every aspect of the analysis Sipe and I had been offering, but which many of them had been previously unwilling to accept.[3]

The debate swirled on in radical therapy circles for several years. Finally, in mid-1985, Sipe, who had by then assumed the editorship of the radical therapy movement's primary organ, *Issues in Radical Therapy*, asked me to write up my thinking on the topic for publication as a major essay in the journal. The result was "Pacifism as Pathology," published in two parts in *IRT*'s winter and spring 1986 issues (Vol.12 Nos 1 and 2.) By 1987, the piece had gone into underground xerox distribution, with several hundred copies circulating in Montréal alone. It also served as the basis for a series of intense philosophical/tactical discussions in locales as diverse as New York, Toronto, Chicago, Seattle, Portland, San Fransisco, Los Angeles, and Atlanta, and was eventually translated into German, French, Spanish, and Arabic.

A lot of water has passed under the bridge since then. The Soviet Union and Yugoslavia have dissolved and Nicaragua's Sandanista revolution has disintegrated. Cuba teeters on the brink of oblivion. East Germany has been absorbed by the West, the former "communist bloc" of eastern Europe has gone capitalist, and both China and Vietnam are trying to do so. The U.S. has bombed

Libya, invaded Panama and Somalia, and all but obliterated Iraq. Armed formations throughout Europe and North America, many of them still quite vibrant at the time "Pacifism" was written, have largely disappeared, their members dead, imprisoned or having defected.[4] To quote George Herbert Walker Bush, a "New World Order" has emerged (which incorporates all the worst aspects of the previous order, only more so).

Domestically in the United States as well, all things positive are in retreat as collaboration between demopublicans and republicrats results in the repeal of each legislatively progressive aspect of U.S. society as far back as the New Deal, the Supreme Court systematically voids even the pretense of constitutional protection and judicial remedy, and the popular wealth is officially transferred at an ever-increasing pace from the poorest to the richest individuals and corporate bodies (not only at home, but from abroad, through instruments like GATT and NAFTA).[5] Hunger and disease stalk the land as they have at no time since the Great Depression of the 1930s while the discontent are sent in their millions into a growing sprawl of newly-constructed prisons, put there by a combination of Bill Clinton's "hundred thousand new cops on the street," a mighty surge in police powers (both authorized and extralegal) and an unprecedented proliferation of repressive technologies.[6]

As even the U.S. labour movement, long a simpering lapdog of government and big business, is dismantled in favour of a kind of corporate profit unheard of since the nineteenth century (or throughout the Third

World), the Steineresque "radicals" – who a generation ago expended so much time and energy preventing the evolution of the kind of revolutionary consciousness, tactics, and strategy which alone could have prevented at least some of this – have come upon "new" agendas for themselves. At the top of their list, as the "opposition's elder statesmen," has been the championing of such "enlightened" measures as "gun control," i.e.: the further empowerment of the state to consumate the sort of complete and unilateral disarmament of the oppressed it has always desired and which they themselves have all along insisted upon.[7]

The hour has indeed grown late, perhaps too late. But then again, maybe not. One thing is certain, however. If the final consolidation of what Bertram Gross somewhat misleadingly referred to as "friendly facism" is not to occur over the next few years, there will have to be a very deep and fundamental rethinking of the kind of "revolutionary" politics which have prevailed in advanced industrial societies, most especially the United States, over the past half-century or more.[8] Consideration of the critique and premises advanced in "Pacifism as Pathology" thus seem more appropriate than ever.

The prospect of republishing the piece has, of course, raised certain questions for me. The fact is that, were I starting from scratch today, I would probably write something very different, retaining the essential themes and perspectives, but developing different emphases and examples, couching my arguments in terms a bit wider of the models that resulted from the original's having emerged from the setting of the now largely defunct radical therapy community. It is nonetheless true that I'm not starting out fresh and that there is something – indeed, very much – to be said for the continuity which attends review of past failures (with an eye toward preventing their recurrence).

Hence, I've opted to leave things pretty much as they were written in 1985, mainly – since I expect much of what is said to resonate with the direct experience of younger readers – as a way of bolstering the extent to which current concerns may be seen as interconnecting with those left unresolved more than a decade ago (just as the essay itself was framed in a manner seeking to connect what was occurring in the early 1980s to what had been occurring ten and twenty years before, and how the thinking of the '60s was – or should have been – tempered by the cataclysmic fates suffered by the Jews, Gypsies, and other passive resisters a generation before *that*). To this end, I've expanded my annotation considerably, partly to provide clarification through citation of a much greater body of literature than was originally the case, partly to amplify a few of the points raised, and partly to rebut certain criticisms which have been raised against my argument (especially those suggesting that to draw uncomfortable lessons from the Holocaust is to be "antisemitic").

The decision to include Mike Ryan's epilogic essay, "On Ward Churchill's 'Pacifism as Pathology'," was also rather natural. Published in the Winter-Spring issue of *IRT* (Vol. XIII, Nos. 1-2), it evolved from notes written a year earlier to form Ryan's side of what was supposed to have been a wide open debate of the issues between himself and a leading advocate of nonviolence during a conference of Canadian radicals. As it turned out, the "other side" of the question not only never produced a publishable – or even coherent – text in response, he contrived to gut the verbal dialogue as well, managing to invoke a conference "rule" limiting his and Ryan's presentation time to fifteen minutes each (shades of the above-mentioned Steinerian maneuver).[9] In any event, the epilogue fills many of the gaps left in my own essay and is a welcome addition to the present volume.

By way of conclusion, I would like to thank Ed Mead for his excellent preface, the unknown author of the poem used as a foreword, and Arbeiter Ring Publishing for having felt it important that this little collection be put forth. Hopefully, *Pacifism as Pathology* will have the effect of contributing to the sort of intellectual/emotional/practical exchange which is so absolutely necessary to the eventual emergence of a truly viable North American praxis, a way of being and doing that is at last capable of transforming that which is into that which could be. If so, it will have been more than worth the effort by all parties concerned.

Notes

1. Post-workshop interview with "Melissa" (tape on file).

2. The quality of the "discussion" which occurred during this event may be measured by Steiner's having asserted at one point that "Churchill is a killer" and "we don't need killers like him conducting workshops on how to kill people." When Sipe inquired as to how he knew I was "a killer," he responded that he "could see it in [my] eyes." This apparently passed as conclusive evidence to most of the radicals in attendance.

3. Upon such grotesque contradictions has many an American movement foundered. RT proved to be no exception. The Midwest Association, which had been growing steadily up to that point, immediately entered a period of stagnation, followed by a steady decline. By the end of the decade it had gone out of existence altogether. Claude Steiner, at the time something of an alternative therapy guru, has also gone into a well-deserved eclipse.

4. An interesting early look at what this means domestically is provided in Donald Stabile, *Prophets of Order: The Rise of the New Class, Technocracy and Socialism in America* (Boston: South End Press, 1984); more lately, see Noam Chomsky, *Class Warfare: Interviews with David Barsamian* (Monroe, ME: Common Courage, 1996). Internationally, see e.g., Noam Chomsky, *Year 501: The Conquest Continues* (Boston: South End, 1993); Micahel Parenti, *Against Empire* (San Fransisco, City Lights, 1995).

5. See, e.g., Charles Andrews, *Profit Fever: The Drive to Corporatize Health Care and How to Stop It* (Monroe, ME: Common Courage, 1995); Michael Hudson, ed., *Merchants of Misery: How Corporate America Profits from Poverty* (Monroe, ME: Common Courage1996); Kevin Danaher, ed., *50 Years is Enough: The Case Against the World Bank and International Monetary Fund* (Boston: South End, 1994).

6. Paul Chevigny, *Edge of the Knife: Police Violence in the Americas* (New York: New Press, 1995); Ward Churchill and J.J. Vander Wall, eds., *Cages of Steel: The Politics of Imprisonment in the United States* (Washington, D.C.: Maisonneuve, 1992).

7. The balance of their script, such as the national pandemic anti-smoking campaigns, have been equally retrograde and diversionary. The common denominator has been a continuous augmentation of state power to regulate ever more nuanced aspects of individual and group behaviour.

The corresponding rate by which common people are *dis*empowered is obvious.

8. Bertram Gross, *Friendly Fascism: The Face of Power in America* (Boston: South End, 1982).

9. It should be noted that, having pronounced the positions taken in "Pacifism as Pathology" to be "absurd," more than an dozen leading proponents of nonviolence comitted themselves at various times between 1986 and 1991 to producing point-by-point written rebuttals for publication. Not one delivered. Instead, apparently unable to come up with convincing arguments of their own, they've uniformly sought to squelch the advancing of alternatives wherever possible.

Pacifism as Pathology:
Notes on an American Psuedopraxis

Ward Churchill

It is the obligation of every person who claims to oppose oppression to resist the oppressor by every means at his or her disposal. Not to engage in physical resistance, armed resistance to oppression, is to serve the interests of the oppressor; no more, no less. There are no exceptions to the rule, no easy out . . .

— Assata Shakur, 1984

Pacifism, the ideology of nonviolent political action, has become axiomatic and all but universal among the more progressive elements of contemporary mainstream North America. With a jargon ranging from a peculiar mishmash of borrowed or fabricated pseudospiritualism to "Gramscian" notions of prefigurative socialization, pacifism appears as the common denominator linking otherwise disparate "white dissident" groupings. Always, it promises that the harsh realities of state power can be transcended via good feelings and purity of purpose rather than by self-defense and resort to combat.

Pacifists, with seemingly endless repetition, pronounce that the negativity of the modern corporate-fascist state will atrophy through defection and neglect once there is a sufficiently positive social vision to take its place ("What if they gave a war and nobody came?"). Known in the Middle Ages as alchemy, such insistence on the repetition of insubstantial themes and failed experiments to obtain a desired result has long been consigned to the realm of fantasy, discarded by all but the most wishful or cynical (who use it to manipulate people).[1]

I don't deny the obviously admirable emotional content of the pacifist perspective. Surely we can all agree that the world should become a place of cooperation, peace, and harmony. Indeed, it *would* be nice if everything would just get better while nobody got hurt, including the oppressor who (temporarily and misguidedly) makes everything bad. Emotional niceties, however, do not render a viable politics. As with most delusions designed to avoid rather than confront unpleasant truths (Lenin's premise that the sort of state he created would wither away under "correct conditions" comes to mind),[2] the pacifist fantasy is inevitably doomed to failure by circumstance.

Even the most casual review of twentieth-century history reveals the graphic contradictions of the pacifist posture, the costs of its continued practice and its fundamental ineffectiveness in accomplishing its purported transformative mission.[3] Nonetheless, we are currently beset by "nonviolent revolutionary leaders" who habitually revise historical fact as a means of offsetting their doctrine's glaring practical deficiencies, and by the spectacle of expressly pacifist organizations claiming (apparently in all seriousness) to be standing "in solidarity" with practitioners of armed resistance in Central America, Africa, and elsewhere.[4]

Despite its inability to avert a revitalized militarism in the United States, the regeneration of overt racism, and a general rise in native fascism, pacifism – the stuff of the spent mass movements of the '60s – not only continues as the normative form of "American activism," but seems to have recently experienced a serious resurgence.[5] The purpose here is to examine the pacifist phenomenon briefly in both its political and psychological dimensions, with an eye toward identifying the relationship between a successful reactionary order on the one hand, and a pacifist domestic opposition on the other.

Like Lambs to the Slaughter

I have never been able to bring myself to trust anyone who claims to have saved a Jew from the SS. The fact is that the Jews were not saved

. . . no one took the steps necessary to save them, even themselves.

– Simon Weisenthal, 1967

Pacifism possesses a sublime arrogance in its implicit assumption that its adherents can somehow dictate the terms of struggle in any contest with the state.[6] Such a supposition seems unaccountable in view of the actual record of passive/nonviolent resistance to state power. Although a number of examples can be mustered with which to illustrate this point – including Buddhist resistance to U.S. policies in Indochina, and the sustained efforts made to terminate white supremacist rule in southern Africa – none seems more appropriate than the Jewish experience in Hitlerian Germany (and later in the whole of occupied Europe).

The record is quite clear that, while a range of pacifist forms of countering the implications of nazism occurred within the German Jewish community during the 1930s, they offered virtually no physical opposition to the consolidation of the nazi state.[7] To the contrary, there is strong evidence that orthodox Jewish leaders counseled "social responsibility" as the best antidote to nazism, while crucial political formulations such as the zionist *Hagana* and *Mossad el Aliyah Bet* actually seem to have attempted to co-opt the nazi agenda for their own purposes, entering into cooperative relations with the SS Jewish Affairs Bureau, and trying to use forced immigration of Jews as a pretext for establishing a "Jewish homeland" in Palestine.[8]

All of this was apparently done in an effort to manipulate the political climate in Germany – by "not exacerbating conditions" and "not alienating the German people any further" – in a manner more favorable to Jews than the nazis were calling for.[9] In the end, of course, the nazis imposed the "final solution to the Jewish question," but by then the dynamics of passive resistance were so entrenched in the Jewish *zeitgeist* (the nazis having been in power a full decade) that a sort of passive accommodation prevailed. Jewish leaders took their people, quietly and nonviolently, first into the ghettos, and then onto trains "evacuating" them to the east. Armed resistance was still widely held to be "irresponsible."[10]

Eventually, the SS could count upon the brunt of the nazi liquidation policy being carried out by the *Sonderkommandos,* which were composed of the Jews themselves. It was largely Jews who dragged the gassed bodies of their exterminated people to the crematoria in death camps such as Auschwitz/Birkenau, each motivated by the desire to prolong his own life. Even this became rationalized as "resistance"; the very act of surviving was viewed as "defeating" the nazi program.[11] By 1945, Jewish passivity and nonviolence in the face of the *weltanschauung der untermenschen* had done nothing to prevent the loss of millions of lives.[12]

The phenomenon sketched above must lead to the obvious question: "[How could] millions of men [*sic*] like us walk to their death without resistance?"[13] In turn, the mere asking of the obvious has spawned a veritable cottage industry among Jewish intellectuals, each explaining how it was that "the process" had left the Jewish people "no choice" but to go along, to remain passive, to proceed in accordance with their aversion to violence right up to the doors of the crematoria – and beyond.[14] From this perspective, there was nothing truly lacking in the Jewish performance; the Jews were simply and solely blameless victims of a genocidal system over which it was quite impossible for them to extend any measure of control.[15]

The Jews having suffered horribly under nazi rule,[16] it has come to be considered in exceedingly poor taste – "antisemitic," according to the logic of the Anti-Defamation League of B'nai Brith – to suggest that there was indeed something very wrong with the nature of the Jewish response to nazism, that the mainly pacifist forms of resistance exhibited by the Jewish community played directly into the hands of their executioners.[17] Objectively, there *were* alternatives, and one need not look to the utterances of some "lunatic fringe" to find them articulated.

Even such a staid and conservative political commentator as Bruno Bettelheim, a former concentration camp inmate, has offered astute analysis of the role of passivity and nonviolence in amplifying the magnitude of the Holocaust. Regarding the single known instance in which inmates physically revolted at Auschwitz, he observes that:

> In the single revolt of the twelfth *Sonderkommando*,
> seventy SS were killed, including one commissioned
> officer and seventeen non-commissioned officers;
> one of the crematoria was totally destroyed and
> another severely damaged. True, all eight hundred
> and fifty-three of the *kommando* died. But . . . the
> one *Sonderkommando* which revolted and took such
> a heavy toll of the enemy did not die much differ-
> ently than all the other *Sonderkommandos*. [18]

Aside from pointing out that the Jews had literally
nothing to lose (and quite a lot to gain in terms of human dignity) by engaging in open revolt against the SS,
Bettelheim goes much further, noting that such actions
both in and outside the death camps stood a reasonable
prospect of greatly impeding the extermination process. [19]
He states flatly that even individualized armed resistance
could have made the Final Solution a cost-prohibitive
proposition for the nazis:

> There is little doubt that the [Jews], who were able
> to provide themselves with so much, could have
> provided themselves with a gun or two had they
> wished. They could have shot down one or two of
> the SS men who came for them. The loss of an SS
> with every Jew arrested would have noticeably hin-
> dered the functioning of the police state. [20]

Returning to the revolt of the twelfth
Sonderkommando, Bettelheim observes that:

> They did only what we should expect all human
> beings to do; to use their death, if they could not

save their lives, to weaken or hinder the enemy as much as possible; to use even their doomed selves for making extermination harder, or maybe impossible, not a smooth-running process . . . If they could do it, so could others. Why didn't they? Why did they throw their lives away instead of making things hard for the enemy? Why did they make a present of their very being to the SS instead of to their families, their friends, even to their fellow prisoners[?][21]

"Rebellion could only have saved either the life they were going to lose anyway, or the lives of others. . . . Inertia it was that led millions of Jews into the ghettos the SS had created for them. It was inertia that made hundreds of thousands of Jews sit home, waiting for their executioners."[22]

Bettelheim describes this inertia, which he considers the basis for Jewish passivity in the face of genocide, as being grounded in a profound desire for "business as usual," the following of rules, the need to not accept reality or to act upon it. Manifested in the irrational belief that in remaining "reasonable and responsible," unobtrusively resisting by continuing "normal" day-to-day activities proscribed by the nazis through the Nuremberg Laws and other infamous legislation, and "not alienating anyone," this attitude implied that a more-or-less humane Jewish policy might be morally imposed upon the nazi state by Jewish pacifism itself.[23]

Thus, Bettelheim continues:

The persecution of the Jews was aggravated, slow step by slow step, when no violent fighting back occurred. It may have been Jewish acceptance, without retaliatory fight, of ever harsher discrimination and degradation that first gave the SS the idea that they could be gotten to the point where they would walk into the gas chambers on their own . . . [I]n the deepest sense, the walk to the gas chamber was only the last consequence of the philosophy of business as usual.[24]

Given this, Bettelheim can do little else but conclude (correctly) that the post-war rationalization and apologia for the Jewish response to nazism serves to "stress how much we all wish to subscribe to this business as usual philosophy, and forget that it hastens our own destruction . . . to glorify the attitude of going on with business as usual, even in a holocaust."[25]

An Essential Contradiction

I have no intention of being a good Jew, led into the ovens like some sheep . . .
— Abbie Hoffman, 1969

The example of the Jews under nazism is, to be sure, extreme. History affords us few comparable models by which to assess the effectiveness of nonviolent opposition to state policies, at least in terms of the scale and rapidity with which consequences were visited upon the passive. Yet it is precisely this extremity which makes the example useful; the Jewish experience reveals with stark clarity the basic illogic at the very core of pacifist conceptions of morality and political action.[26]

Proponents of nonviolent political "praxis" are inherently placed in the position of claiming to meet the armed might of the state via an asserted moral superiority attached to the renunciation of arms and physical violence altogether. It follows that the state has demonstrated, *a priori*, its fundamental immorality/illegitimacy by arming itself in the first place. A certain psychological correlation is typically offered wherein the "good" and "positive" social vision (*Eros*) held by the pacifist opposition is posed against the "bad" or "negative" realities (*Thanatos*) evidenced by the state. The correlation lends itself readily to "good versus evil" dichotomies, fostering a view of social conflict as a morality play.[27]

There can be no question but that there is a superficial logic to the analytical equation thus established. The Jews in their disarmed and passive resistance to German oppression during the '30s and '40s were certainly "good"; the nazis – as well-armed as any group in history up to that point – might undoubtedly be assessed as a force of unmitigated "evil."[28] Such binary correlations might also be extended to describe other sets of historical forces: Gandhi's Indian Union (good) versus troops of the British Empire (evil) and Martin Luther King's nonviolent Civil Rights Movement (good) versus a host of Klansmen and Southern cracker police (evil) offer ready examples.

In each case, the difference between them can be (and often is) attributed to the relative willingness/unwillingness of the opposing sides to engage in violence. And, in each case, it can be (and has been) argued that good ultimately overcame the evil it confronted, achieving political gains and at least temporarily dissipating a form of social violence. To the extent that Eichmann was eventually tried in Jerusalem for his part in the genocide of the Jewish people, that India has passed from the control of England, and that Mississippi blacks can now register to vote with comparative ease, it may be (and is) contended that there is a legacy of nonviolent political success informing the praxis of contemporary pacifism.[29]

It becomes quite possible for sensitive, refined, and morally developed individuals to engage in socially transformative political action while rejecting violence (*per se*) as a means or method containing a positive as well as negative utility. The teleological assumption here is that a sort of "negation of the negation" is involved, that the "power of nonviolence" can in itself be used to supplant the offending societal violence represented in the formation of state power. The key to the whole is that *it has been done*, as the survival of at least some of the Jews, the decolonization of India, and the enfranchisement of Southern American blacks demonstrate.[30]

This tidy scheme, pleasing as it may be on an emotional level, brings up more questions than it answers. An obvious question is that if nonviolence is to be taken as the emblem of Jewish goodness in the face of nazi evil, how is one to account for the revolt of the twelfth *Sonderkommando* mentioned by Bettelheim, or scattered incidents of the same type which occurred at other death camps such as Sobibór and Treblinka.[31] What of the several thousand participants in the sole mass uprising of Jews outside the camps, the armed revolt of the Warsaw Ghetto during April and May 1943?[32] May it rightly be suggested that those who took up arms against their executioners crossed the same symbolic line demarcating good and evil, becoming "the same" as the SS?[33]

One may assume for the moment that such a gross distortion of reality is hardly the intent of even the hardiest pacifist polemicists, although it may well be an intrinsic aspect of their position. Worse than this is the inconsistency of nonviolent premises. For instance, it has been abundantly documented that nazi policy toward the Jews, from 1941 onward, was bound up in the notion that extermination would proceed until such time as the entire Jewish population within German occupied territory was liquidated.[34] There is no indication whatsoever that nonviolent intervention/mediation from any quarter held the least prospect of halting, or even delaying, the genocidal process. To the contrary, there is evidence that efforts by neutral parties such as the Red Cross had the effect of *speeding up* the slaughter.[35]

That the Final Solution was halted at a point short of its full realization was due solely to the massive application of armed force against Germany (albeit for reasons other than the salvation of the Jews). Left to a pacifist prescription for the altering of offensive state policies, and the effecting of positive social change, "World Jewry" – at least in its Eurasian variants – would have suffered total extermination by mid-1946 at the latest. Even the highly symbolic trial of SS Colonel Adolph Eichmann could not be accomplished by nonviolent means, but required armed action by an Israeli paramilitary unit fifteen years after the last death camp was closed by Russian tanks.[36] There is every indication that adherence to pacifist principles would have resulted in Eichmann's permanent avoidance of justice, living out his life in reasonable comfort until – to paraphrase his own assessment – he leapt into the grave laughing at the thought of having killed six million Jews.[37] With reference to the Jewish experience, nonviolence was a catastrophic failure, and only the most extremely violent intervention by others saved Europe's Jews at the last moment from slipping over the brink of utter extinction. Small wonder that the survivors insist, "Never again!"

While other examples are less crystalline in their implications, they are instructive. The vaunted career of Gandhi exhibits characteristics of a calculated strategy of nonviolence salvaged only by the existence of violent peripheral processes.[38] While it is true that the great Indian leader never deviated from his stance of passive resistance to British colonization, and that in the end England found it cost-prohibitive to continue its effort to assert control in the face of his opposition, it is equally true that the Gandhian success must be viewed in the context of a general decline in British power brought about by two world wars within a thirty-year period.[39]

Prior to the decimation of British troop strength and the virtual bankruptcy of the Imperial treasury during World War II, Gandhi's movement showed little likelihood of forcing England's abandonment of India. Without the global violence that destroyed the Empire's ability to forcibly control its colonial territories (and passive populations), India might have continued indefinitely in the pattern of minority rule marking the majority of South Africa's modern history, the first locale in which the Gandhian recipe for liberation struck the reef of reality.[40] Hence, while the Mahatma and his followers were able to remain "pure," their victory was contingent upon others physically gutting their opponents for them.

Similarly, the limited success attained by Martin Luther King and his disciples in the United States during the 1960s, using a strategy consciously guided by Gandhian principles of nonviolence, owes a considerable debt to the existence of less pacifist circumstances. King's movement had attracted considerable celebrity, but precious little in the way of tangible political gains prior to the emergence of a trend signaled in 1967 by the redesignation of the Student Nonviolent Coordinating Committee (SNCC; more or less the campus arm of King's Civil Rights Movement) as the Student *National* Coordinating Committee.[41]

The SNCC's action (precipitated by non-pacifists such as Stokely Carmichael and H. Rap Brown) occurred in the context of armed self-defense tactics being employed for the first time by rural black leaders such as Robert Williams, and the eruption of black urban enclaves in Detroit, Newark, Watts, Harlem, and elsewhere. It also coincided with the increasing need of the American state for internal stability due to the unexpectedly intense and effective armed resistance mounted by the Vietnamese against U.S. aggression in Southeast Asia.[42]

Suddenly King, previously stonewalled and redbaited by the establishment, his roster of civil rights demands evaded or dismissed as being "too radical" and "premature," found himself viewed as the lesser of evils by the state.[43] He was duly anointed *the* "responsible black leader" in the media, and his cherished civil rights agenda was largely incorporated into law during 1968 (along with appropriate riders designed to neutralize "Black Power Militants" such as Carmichael, Brown, and Williams.)[44] Without the spectre, real or perceived, of a violent black revolution at large in America during a time of war, King's nonviolent strategy was basically impotent in concrete terms. As one of his Northern organizers, William Jackson, put it to me in 1969:

> There are a lot of reasons why I can't get behind fomenting violent actions like riots, and *none* of 'em are religious. It's all pragmatic politics. But I'll tell you what: I *never* let a riot slide by. I'm always the first one down at city hall and testifying before Congress, tellin' 'em, "See? If you guys'd been dealing with *us* all along, this never would have hap-

pened." It gets results, man. Like nothin' else, y'know? The thing is that Rap Brown and the Black Panthers are just about the best things that ever happened to the Civil Rights Movement.

Jackson's exceedingly honest, if more than passingly cynical, outlook was tacitly shared by King.[45] The essential contradiction inherent to pacifist praxis is that, for survival itself, any nonviolent confrontation of state power must ultimately depend either on the state refraining from unleashing some real measure of its potential violence, or the active presence of some counterbalancing violence of precisely the sort pacifism professes to reject as a political option.

Absurdity clearly abounds when suggesting that the state will refrain from using all necessary physical force to protect against undesired forms of change and threats to its safety. Nonviolent tacticians imply (perhaps unwittingly) that the "immoral state" which they seek to transform will somehow exhibit exactly the same sort of *superior* morality they claim for themselves (i.e., at least a relative degree of nonviolence). The fallacy of such a proposition is best demonstrated by the nazi state's removal of its "Jewish threat."[46]

Violent intervention by others divides itself naturally into the two parts represented by Gandhi's unsolicited "windfall" of massive violence directed against his opponents and King's rather more conscious and deliberate utilization of incipient antistate violence as a means of advancing his own pacifist agenda. History is replete with variations on these two subthemes, but variations do little to alter the crux of the situation: there simply has never been a revolution, or even a substantial social reorganization, brought into being on the basis of the principles of pacifism.[47] In every instance, violence has been an integral *requirement* of the process of transforming the state.

Pacifist praxis (or, more appropriately, pseudopraxis), if followed to its logical conclusions, leaves its adherents with but two possible outcomes to their line of action:

1. To render themselves perpetually ineffectual (and consequently unthreatening) in the face of state power, in which case they will likely be largely ignored by the status quo and self-eliminating in terms of revolutionary potential; or,

2. To make themselves a clear and apparent danger to the state, in which case they are subject to physical liquidation by the status quo and are self-eliminating in terms of revolutionary potential.

In either event – mere ineffectuality or suicide – the objective conditions leading to the necessity for social revolution remain unlikely to be altered by purely pacifist strategies. As these conditions typically include war, the induced starvation of whole populations and the like, pacifism and its attendant sacrifice of life cannot even be rightly said to have substantially impacted the level of evident societal violence. The mass suffering that revolution is intended to alleviate will continue as the revolution strangles itself on the altar of "nonviolence."

The Comfort Zone

Don't speak to me of revolution until you're
ready to eat rats to survive . . .
                                    – The Last Poets, 1972

Regardless of the shortcomings of pacifism as a methodological approach to revolution, there is nothing inherent in its basic impulse which prevents real practitioners from experiencing the revolutionary ethos. Rather, as already noted, the emotional content of the principle of nonviolence is tantamount to a gut-level rejection of much, or even all, that the present social order stands for – an intrinsically revolutionary perspective. The question is not the motivations of real pacifists, but instead the nature of a strategy by which the revolution may be won, at a minimum sacrifice to all concerned.

This assumes that sacrifice is being made by *all* concerned. Here, it becomes relatively easy to separate the wheat from the chaff among America's proponents of "nonviolent opposition." While the premise of pacifism necessarily precludes engaging in violent acts directed at others, even for reasons of self-defense, it does not prevent its adherents from themselves incurring physical punishment in pursuit of social justice. In other words,

there is nothing of a doctrinal nature barring real pacifists from running real risks.

And indeed they do. Since at least the early Chris-
tians, devout pacifists have been sacrificing themselves
while standing up for what they believe in against the
armed might of those they consider wrong. Gandhi's followers perished by the thousands, allowed themselves to
be beaten and maimed *en masse*, and clogged India's pe-
nal system in their campaign to end British rule.[48] King's
field organizers showed incredible bravery in confronting the racist thugs of the South, and many paid with
their lives on lonely back roads.[49]

Another type of pacifist action which became a sym-
bol for the nonviolent antiwar movement was that of a
Buddhist monk, Thich Quang Duc, who immolated himself on a Saigon street on June 11, 1963. Duc's protest
against growing U.S. involvement in his country was
quickly followed by similar actions by other Vietnamese
bonzes and, on November 2, 1965, by an American
Quaker, Norman Morrison, who burned himself in front
of the Pentagon to protest increasing levels of U.S. troop
commitment in Indochina.[50] Whatever the strategic value
one may place upon the actions of Morrison and the
Buddhists – and it must be acknowledged that the U.S.
grip on Vietnam rapidly *tightened* after the self-immolations began,[51] while U.S. troop strength in Southeast Asia
spiraled from some 125,000 at the time of Morrison's
suicide to more than 525,000 barely two years later –
they were unquestionably courageous people, entirely

willing to face the absolute certainty of the most excruci-
ating death in pursuit of their professed ideals. Although
the effectiveness of their tactics is open to question, their
courage and integrity certainly are not.

In a less severe fashion, there are many other examples of American pacifists putting themselves on the line
for their beliefs. The Berrigan brothers, Phillip and Daniel, clearly qualify in this regard, as do a number of others who took direct action against the Selective Service
System and certain U.S. military targets during the late
'60s and early '70s.[52] Cadres of Witness for Peace placed
their bodies between CIA-sponsored contra guerrillas and
their intended civilian victims along the Nicaragua/Hon-
duras border during the '80s.[53] Members of Greenpeace,
Earth First!, and Friends of the Earth have been known
to take considerable chances with their own well-being
in their advocacy of a range of environmental issues.[54]

The list of principled and self-sacrificing pacifists
and pacifist acts could undoubtedly be extended and,
ineffectual or not, these people are admirable in their
own right. Unfortunately, they represent the exception
rather than the rule of pacifist performance in the United
States. For every example of serious and committed pacifist activism emerging from the normative mass of American nonviolent movements since 1965, one could cite
scores of countering instances in which only lip service
was paid to the ideals of action and self-sacrifice.

The question central to the emergence and maintenance of nonviolence as the oppositional foundation

of American activism has not been the truly pacifist formulation, "How can we forge a revolutionary politics within which we can avoid inflicting violence on others?" On the contrary, a more accurate guiding question has been, "What sort of politics might I engage in which will both allow me to posture as a progressive *and* allow me to avoid incurring harm to *myself*?" Hence, the trappings of pacifism have been subverted to establish a sort of "politics of the comfort zone," not only akin to what Bettelheim termed "the philosophy of business as usual" and devoid of perceived risk to its advocates, but minus any conceivable revolutionary impetus as well.[55] The intended revolutionary content of true pacifist activism – the sort practiced by the Gandhian movement, the Berrigans, and Norman Morrison – is thus isolated and subsumed in the United States, even among the ranks of self-professing participants.

Such a situation must abort whatever limited utility pacifist tactics might have, absent other and concurrent forms of struggle, as a socially transformative method. Yet the history of the American Left over the past decade shows too clearly that the more diluted the substance embodied in "pacifist practice," the louder the insistence of its subscribers that nonviolence is the *only* mode of action "appropriate and acceptable within the context of North America," and the greater the effort to ostracize, or even stifle divergent types of actions.[56] Such strategic hegemony exerted by proponents of this truncated range of tactical options has done much to foreclose on whatever revolutionary potential may be said to exist in modern America.

Is such an assessment too harsh? One need only attend a mass demonstration (ostensibly directed against the policies of the state) in any U.S. city to discover the answer. One will find hundreds, sometimes thousands, assembled in orderly fashion, listening to selected speakers calling for an end to this or that aspect of lethal state activity, carrying signs "demanding" the same thing, welcoming singers who enunciate lyrically on the worthiness of the demonstrators' agenda as well as the plight of the various victims they are there to "defend," and – typically – the whole thing is quietly disbanded with exhortations to the assembled to "keep working" on the matter and to please sign a petition and/or write letters to congresspeople requesting that they alter or abandon offending undertakings.

Throughout the whole charade it will be noticed that the state is represented by a uniformed police presence keeping a discreet distance and not interfering with the activities. And why should they? The organizers of the demonstration will have gone through "proper channels" to obtain permits *required by the state* and instructions as to where they will be allowed to assemble, how long they will be allowed to stay and, should a march be involved in the demonstration, along which routes they will be allowed to walk.

Surrounding the larger mass of demonstrators can be seen others – an élite. Adorned with green (or white, or powder blue) armbands, their function is to ensure that demonstrators remain "responsible," not deviating from the state-sanctioned plan of protest. Individuals or small groups who attempt to spin off from the main body, entering areas to which the state has denied access (or some other unapproved activity) are headed off by these armbanded "marshals" who argue – pointing to the nearby police – that "troublemaking" will only "exacerbate an already tense situation" and "provoke violence," thereby "alienating those we are attempting to reach."[57] In some ways, the voice of the "good Jews" can be heard to echo plainly over the years.

At this juncture, the confluence of interests between the state and the mass nonviolent movement could not be clearer. The role of the police, whose function is to support state policy by minimizing disruption of its procedures, should be in natural conflict with that of a movement purporting to challenge these same policies and, indeed, to transform the state itself.[58] However, with apparent perverseness, the police find themselves serving as mere backups (or props) to *self*-policing (now euphemistically termed "peace-keeping" rather than the more accurate "marshaling") efforts of the alleged opposition's own membership. Both sides of the "contestation" concur that the smooth functioning of state processes must not be physically disturbed, at least not in any significant way.[59]

All of this is within the letter and spirit of cooptive forms of sophisticated self-preservation appearing as an integral aspect of the later phases of bourgeois democracy.[60] It dovetails well with more shopworn methods such as the electoral process and has been used by the state as an innovative means of conducting public opinion polls, which better hide rather than eliminate controversial policies.[61] Even the movement's own sloganeering tends to bear this out from time to time, as when Students for a Democratic Society (SDS) coined the catch-phrase of its alternative to the polling place: "Vote with your feet, vote in the street."[62]

Of course, any movement seeking to project a credible self-image as something other than just one more variation of accommodation to state power must ultimately establish its "militant" oppositional credentials through the media in a manner more compelling than rhetorical speechifying and the holding of impolite placards ("Fuck the War" was always a good one) at rallies.[63] Here, the time-honored pacifist notion of "civil disobedience" is given a new twist by the adherents of nonviolence in America. Rather than pursuing Gandhi's (or, to a much lesser extent, King's) method of using passive bodies to literally clog the functioning of the state apparatus – regardless of the cost to those doing the clogging – the American nonviolent movement has increasingly opted for "symbolic actions."[64]

The centerpiece of such activity usually involves an arrest, either of a token figurehead of the movement (or a small, selected group of them) or a mass arrest of some sort. In the latter event, "arrest training" is generally provided – and lately has become "required" by movement organizers – by the same marshals who will later ensure that crowd control police units will be left with little or nothing to do. This is to ensure that "no one gets hurt" in the process of being arrested, and that the police are not inconvenienced by disorganized arrest procedures.[65]

The event which activates the arrests is typically preplanned, well-publicized in advance, and, more often than not, literally coordinated with the police – often including estimates by organizers concerning how many arrestees will likely be involved. Generally speaking, such "extreme statements" will be scheduled to coincide with larger-scale peaceful demonstrations so that a considerable audience of "committed" bystanders (and, hopefully, NBC/CBS/ABC/CNN) will be on hand to applaud the bravery and sacrifice of those arrested; most of the bystanders will, of course, have considered reasons why they themselves are unprepared to "go so far" as to be arrested.[66] The specific sort of action designed to precipitate the arrests themselves usually involves one of the following: (a) sitting down in a restricted area and refusing to leave when ordered; (b) stepping across an imaginary line drawn on the ground by a police representative; (c) refusing to disperse at the appointed time; or (d) chaining or padlocking the doors to a public building. When things *really* get heavy, those seeking to be arrested may pour blood (real or ersatz) on something of "symbolic value."[67]

As a rule, those arrested are cooperative in the ex-

treme, meekly allowing police to lead them to waiting
vans or buses for transportation to whatever station house
or temporary facility has been designated as the process-
ing point. In especially "militant" actions, arrestees go
limp, undoubtedly severely taxing the state's repressive
resources by forcing the police to carry them bodily to
the vans or buses (monitored all the while by volunteer
attorneys who are there to ensure that such "police brutality" as pushing, shoving, or dropping an arrestee does
not occur). In either event, the arrestees sit quietly in
their assigned vehicles – or sing "We Shall Overcome"
and other favourites – as they are driven away for book-
ing. The typical charges levied will be trespassing, creating a public disturbance, or being a public nuisance. In
the heavy instances, the charge may be escalated to mali-
cious mischief or even destruction of public property.
Either way, other than in exceptional circumstances, everyone will be assigned an arraignment date and released
on personal recognizance or a small cash bond, home in
time for dinner (and to review their exploits on the six
o'clock news).[68]

In the unlikely event that charges are not dismissed
prior to arraignment (the state having responded to symbolic actions by engaging largely in symbolic selective
prosecutions), the arrestee will appear on the appointed
date in a room resembling a traffic court where s/he will
be allowed to plead guilty, pay a minimal fine, and go
home. Repeat offenders may be "sentenced" to pay a
somewhat larger fine (which, of course, goes into state

accounts underwriting the very policies the arrestees ostensibly oppose) or even to perform a specific number of "public service hours" (promoting police/community relations, for example).[69] It is almost unheard of for arrestees to be sentenced to jail time for the simple reason that most jails are already overflowing with less principled individuals, most of them rather unpacifist in nature, and many of whom have caused the state a considerably greater degree of displeasure than the nonviolent movement, which claims to seek its radical alteration.[70]

For those arrestees who opt to plead not-guilty to the charges they themselves literally arranged to incur, a trial date will be set. They will thereby accrue another symbolic advantage by exercising their right to explain why they did whatever they did before a judge and jury. They may then loftily contend that it is the state, rather than themselves, that is really criminal. Their rights satisfied, they will then generally be sentenced to exactly the same penalty which would have been levied had they pleaded guilty at their arraignment (plus court costs), and go home. A few will be sentenced to a day or two in jail as an incentive not to waste court time with such pettiness in the future. A few less will refuse to pay whatever fine is imposed, and receive as much as thirty days in jail (usually on work release) as an alternative; a number of these have opted to pen "prison letters" during the period of their brief confinement, underscoring the sense of symbolic (rather than literal) self-sacrifice which is sought.[71]

The trivial nature of this level of activity does not come fully into focus until it is juxtaposed to the sorts of state activity which the nonviolent movement claims to be "working on." A brief sampling of prominent issues addressed by the American opposition since 1965 will suffice for purposes of illustration: the U.S. escalation of the ground war in Southeast Asia to a level where more than a million lives were lost, the saturation bombing of Vietnam (another one to two million killed), the expansion of the Vietnam war into all of Indochina (costing perhaps another two to three million lives when the intentional destruction of Cambodia's farmland and resultant mass starvation are considered), U.S. sponsorship of the Pinochet coup in Chile (at least another 10,000 dead), U.S. underwriting of the Salvadoran oligarchy (50,000 lives at a minimum), U.S. support of the Guatemalan junta (perhaps 200,000 killed since 1954), and efforts to destabilize the Sandinista government in Nicaragua (at least 20,000 dead).[72] A far broader sample of comparably lethal activities has gone unopposed altogether.[73]

While the human costs of continuing American business as usual have registered well into the seven-digit range (and possibly higher), the nonviolent "opposition" in the United States has not only restricted its tactics almost exclusively to the symbolic arena denoted above, but has actively endeavored to prevent others from going further. The methods employed to this end have generally been restricted to the deliberate stigmatizing, isolation, and minimization of other potentials – as a means of neutralizing, or at least containing them – although at times it seems to have crossed over into collaboration with state efforts to bring about their outright liquidation.[74]

The usual approach has been a consistent *a priori* dismissal of any one person or group attempting to move beyond the level of symbolic action as "abandoning the original spirit [of North American oppositional politics] and taking the counterproductive path of small-scale violence now and organizing for serious armed struggle later."[75] This is persistently coupled with attempts to diminish the importance of actions aimed at concrete rather than symbolic effects, epitomized in the question framed by Sam Brown, a primary organizer of the November 1969 Moratorium to End the War in Vietnam (when perhaps 5,000 broke free of a carefully orchestrated schedule of passive activities): "What's more important, that a bunch of scruffy people charged the Justice Department, or that [500,000 people] were in the same place at one time to sing?"[76]

Not only was such "violence" as destroying property and scuffling with police proscribed in the view of the Moratorium organizers, but also any tendency to utilize the incredible mass of assembled humanity in any way which might tangibly interfere with the smooth physical functioning of the governing apparatus in the nation's capital (e.g., nonviolent civil disobedience on the order of, say, systematic traffic blockages and huge sit-ins).[77]

Unsurprisingly, this same mentality manifested it-self even more clearly a year and a half later with the open boycott by pacifism's "responsible leadership" (and most of their committed followers) of the Indochina Peace Campaign's planned "May Day Demonstration" in Washington. Despite the fact that in some ways the war had escalated (e.g., increasingly heavy bombing) since the largest symbolic protest in American history – the Moratorium fielded approximately *one million* passive demonstrators, nationwide – it was still held that May Day organizer Rennie Davis' intent to "show the govern-ment that it will no longer be able to control its own society unless it ends the war NOW!" was "going too far." It was opined that although the May Day plan did not itself call for violent acts, its disruption of business as usual was likely to "provoke a violent response from officials."[78]

Even more predictably, advocates of nonviolence felt compelled to counter such emergent trends as the SDS Revolutionary Youth Movement, Youth Against War and Fascism, and Weatherman.[79] Calling for non-attend-ance at the demonstrations of "irresponsible" organiza-tions attempting to build a "fighting movement among white radicals," and wittily coining derogatory phrases to describe them, the oppositional mainstream did its utmost to thwart possible positive developments coming from such unpacifist quarters. In the end, the stigma-tized organizations themselves institutionalized this im-posed isolation, their frustration with attempting to break the inertia of symbolic opposition to the status quo converted into a "politics of despair" relying solely on violent actions undertaken by a network of tiny underground cells.[80]

The *real* anathema to the nonviolent mass, however, turned out not to be white splinter groups such as Weatherman. Rather, it came from a militant black nationalism embodied in the Black Panther Party for Self-Defense. After nearly a decade of proclaiming its "absolute solidarity" with the liberatory efforts of American blacks, pacifism found itself confronted during the late '60s with the appearance of a cohesive organization that consciously linked the oppression of the black community to the exploitation of people the world over, and *programmatically* asserted the same right to armed self-defense acknowledged as the due of liberation movements abroad.[81]

As the Panthers evidenced signs of making significant headway, organizing first in their home community of Oakland and then nationally, the state perceived something more threatening than yet another series of candlelight vigils. It reacted accordingly, targeting the Panthers for physical elimination. When Party cadres responded (as promised) by meeting the violence of repression with armed resistance, the bulk of their "principled" white support evaporated. This horrifying retreat rapidly isolated the Party from any possible mediating or buffering from the full force of state terror and left its members nakedly exposed to "surgical termination" by special police units.[82]

To cover this default on true pacifist principles – which call upon adherents not to run for safety but, in the manner of Witness for Peace, to interpose their bodies as a means of alleviating violence – it became fashionable to observe that the Panthers were "as bad as the cops" in that they had resorted to arms (a view which should give pause when one recalls the twelfth *Sonderkommando*); they had "brought this on themselves" when they "provoked violence" by refusing the state an uncontested right to maintain the lethal business as usual it had visited upon black America since the inception of the Republic.[83]

In deciphering the meaning of this pattern of response to groups such as the Panthers, Weatherman, and others who have attempted to go beyond a more symbolic protest of, say, genocide, it is important to look behind the clichés customarily used to explain the American pacifist posture (however revealing these may be in themselves). More to the point than concerns that the groups such as the Panthers "bring this [violent repression] on themselves" is the sentiment voiced by Irv Kurki, a prominent Illinois anti-draft organizer during the winter of 1969-70:

> This idea of armed struggle or armed self-defense or whatever you want to call it . . . practiced by the Black Panther Party, the Weathermen and a few other groups is a very bad scene, a really dangerous thing for all of us. This isn't Algeria or Vietnam, it's the United States . . . these tactics are not only coun-

terproductive in that they alienate people who are otherwise very sympathetic to us . . . and lead to the sort of thing which just happened in Chicago . . . but *they run the very real risk of bringing the same sort of violent repression down on all of us* (emphasis added).[84]

Precisely. The preoccupation with avoiding actions which might "provoke violence" is thus not based on a sincere belief that violence will, or even can, truly be avoided. Pacifists, no less than their unpacifist counterparts, are quite aware that violence *already* exists as an integral component in the execution of state policies and requires no provocation; this is a formative basis of their doctrine. What is at issue then cannot be a valid attempt to stave off or even minimize violence *per se*. Instead, it can only be a conscious effort not to refocus state violence in such a way that it would directly impact American pacifists *themselves*. This is true even when it can be shown that the tactics which could trigger such a refocusing might in themselves alleviate a real measure of the much more massive state-inflicted violence occurring elsewhere; better that another 100,000 Indochinese peasants perish under a hail of cluster bombs and napalm than America's principled progressives suffer real physical pain while rendering their government's actions impracticable.[85]

Such conscientious avoidance of personal sacrifice (i.e., dodging the experience of being on the receiving end of violence, *not* the inflicting of it) has nothing to do with the lofty ideals and integrity by which American pacifists claim to inform their practice. But it does explain the real nature of such curious phenomena as movement marshals, steadfast refusals to attempt to bring the seat of government to a standstill even when a million people are on hand to accomplish the task, and the consistently convoluted victim-blaming engaged in with regard to domestic groups such as the Black Panther Party.[86] Massive and unremitting violence in the colonies is appalling to right-thinking people but ultimately acceptable when compared with the unthinkable alternative that any degreee of real violence might be redirected against "mother country radicals."[87]

Viewed in this light, a great many things make sense. For instance, the persistent use of the term "responsible leadership" in describing the normative non-violent sector of North American dissent – always somewhat mysterious when applied to supposed radicals (or German Jews) – is clarified as signifying nothing substantially different from the accommodation of the status quo it implies in more conventional settings.[88] The "rules of the game" have long been established and tacitly agreed to by both sides of the ostensible "oppositional equation": demonstrations of "resistance" to state policies will be allowed so long as they do nothing to materially interfere with the implementation of those policies.[89]

The responsibility of the oppositional leadership in such a trade-off is to ensure that state processes are not threatened by substantial physical disruption; the reciprocal responsibility of the government is to guarantee the general safety of those who play according to the rules.[90] This comfortable scenario is enhanced by the mutual understanding that certain levels of "appropriate" (symbolic) protest of given policies will result in the "oppositional victory" of their modification (i.e., really a "tuning" of policy by which it may be rendered more functional and efficient, *never* an abandonment of fundamental policy thrusts), while efforts to move beyond this metaphorical medium of dissent will be squelched "by any means necessary" and by *all* parties concerned.[91] Meanwhile, the entire unspoken arrangement is larded with a layer of stridently abusive rhetoric directed by each side against the other.

We are left with a husk of opposition, a ritual form capable of affording a sentimentalistic "I'm OK, you're OK" satisfaction to its subscribers at a psychic level but utterly useless in terms of transforming the power relations perpetuating systemic global violence. Such a defect can, however, be readily sublimated within the aggregate comfort zone produced by the continuation of North American business as usual; those who remain within the parameters of nondisruptive dissent allowed by the state, their symbolic duty to the victims of U.S. policy done (and with the bases of state power wholly unchallenged), can devote themselves to the prefiguration of the revolutionary future society with which they proclaim they will replace the present social order (having, no doubt, persuaded the state to overthrow itself through the moral force of their arguments).[92] Here, concrete activities such as sexual experimentation, refinement of musical/artistic tastes, development of various meat-free diets, getting in touch with one's "id" through meditation and ingestion of hallucinogens, alteration of sex-based distribution of household chores, and waging campaigns against such "bourgeois vices" as smoking tobacco become the signifiers of "correct politics" or even "revolutionary practice." This is *as opposed to* the active and effective confrontation of state power.[93]

Small wonder that North America's ghetto, barrio, and reservation populations, along with the bulk of the white working class – people who are by and large structurally denied access to the comfort zone (both in material terms and in a corresponding inability to avoid the imposition of a relatively high degree of systemic violence) – tend either to stand aside in bemused incomprehension of such politics or to react with outright hostility. Their apprehension of the need for revolutionary change and their conception of revolutionary dynamics are necessarily at radical odds with this notion of "struggle."[94] The American nonviolent movement, which has laboured so long and so hard to isolate all divergent oppositional tendencies, is in the end isolating itself, becoming ever more demographically white, middle-class, and "respectable." Eventually, unless there is a marked change in its obstinate insistence that it holds a "moral right" to absolute tactical monopoly, American pacifism will be left to "feel good about itself" while the revolution goes on without it.[95]

Let's Pretend

*Are you listening Nixon? Johnson refused to
hear us, and you know what happened to that
ol' boy . . .*

— Benjamin Spock, 1969

American pacifism seeks to project itself as a revolutionary alternative to the status quo.[96] Of course, such a movement or perspective can hardly acknowledge that its track
record in forcing substantive change upon the state has
been an approximate zero. A chronicle of significant success must be offered, even where none exists. Equally,
should such a movement or perspective seek hegemony
of its particular vision – again, as American pacifism has
been shown to do since 1965 – a certain mythological
complex is required to support its contentions. Generally speaking, both needs can be accommodated within a
single unified propaganda structure.[97]

For proponents of the hegemony of nonviolent
political action within the American opposition, time-
honored fables such as the success of Gandhi's methods
(in and of themselves) and even the legacy of Martin
Luther King no longer retain the freshness and vitality
required to achieve the necessary result. As this has become increasingly apparent, and as the potential to bring

a number of emergently dissident elements (e.g., "freez-ers," antinukers, environmentalists, opponents to saber-rattling in Central America and the Mideast, and so on) into some sort of centralized mass movement became greater in the mid-80s, a freshly packaged pacifist "his-tory" of its role in opposing the Vietnam war began to be peddled with escalating frequency and insistence.[98] It is instructive to examine several salient claims still extended by pacifist organizers.

The nonviolent mass movement against the war forced Lyndon Johnson from office when he failed to with-draw from Vietnam (picking up a theme topical to the antiwar movement itself). Actually, as has been conclu-sively demonstrated, it was "Hawks" rather than "Doves" who toppled Johnson.[99] This was due to the perceived ineffectiveness with which he prosecuted the war, brought about not by pacifist parades in American streets, but by the effectiveness of *Vietnamese armed resistance* to the U.S. military. The catalyst was the Vietnamese Tet Offensive in January 1968 after U.S. Commanding General William Westmoreland announced he had "broken their ability to fight," and the general's resultant request for another 206,000 troops to augment the more than one-half million men already at his disposal.[100] At this point, the *right wing* decided that the war was lost and to begin a process of cutting losses, thereby forcing Johnson out.

To discern where the balance of power lay and be-gin to unravel who did what to whom, one need only look at the fact that the antiwar candidate of the 1968

campaign (Eugene McCarthy) was never in serious contention as Johnson's replacement, and that it was the
choice of the right (Richard Nixon) who became the suc-
cessor.[101]

**The self-sacrifice of such nonviolent oppositional tac-
tics as draft resistance seriously impaired the functioning of the U.S. military machine** (picking up another
topical theme). Actually, there was not much self-sacrifice or risk involved. Of the estimated one million American males who committed draft offenses during the Vietnam era, only 25,000 (2.5 percent) were indicted, and
a total of 3,250 (0.3 percent) went to prison. As many as
80,000 went into voluntary exile in Canada where they
noted the penalty of "being lonely."[102] The other 91.5
percent of these self-sacrificing individuals apparently paid
no price at all, remaining in the comfort zone relative to
both the military and the supposed consequences of evad-
ing it.

It may be that draft resistance on this scale somehow affected the *reserve* manpower of the military but
not its main force units. What *did* affect the functioning
of the military was the rapid disintegration of morale
among U.S. combat troops after 1968 as a result of the
effectiveness of Vietnamese *armed* resistance. The degeneration of effectiveness within the U.S. military, which
eventually neutralized it in the field, included mass refusal to fight (approved, undoubtedly, by pacifists),
spiraling substance abuse (ditto), and, most effectively,
the assassination of commissioned and noncommissioned

officers (well, that's going too far).[103]

The most effective tactic the nonviolent movement could have engaged in to impair the U.S. military was therefore the one thing it was most unprepared to consider: making the individual personal sacrifice of going *into* the military in a massive way in order to quickly subvert it.

The nonviolent mass antiwar movement's solidarity with the Vietnamese undercut the political ability of the U.S. government to continue and forced the war to an early close (a stated objective of the movement of the late '60s). This claim is obviously closely akin to the contention concerning Johnson, although it should be recalled that even U.S. ground forces remained in Vietnam for another four years after that "victory." Actually, there was no mass antiwar movement in the United States, nonviolent or otherwise, by the time the war ended in 1975. It had begun to dissipate rapidly during the summer of 1970 in the wake of sustaining its first and only real casualties – a total of four dead at Kent State University in Ohio that spring.[104] By the time the last U.S. ground troops were withdrawn in 1973, Nixinger had suspended the draft, and with the element of their personal jeopardy thus eliminated, the "principled" opposition fueling the mass movement evaporated altogether while the war did not.

That the war then continued for another three years with U.S. technological and economic support at the cost of hundreds of thousands of Vietnamese lives but absent even a symbolic mass American opposition worthy of the name says volumes about the nature of the nonviolent movement's "solidarity with the Vietnamese."[105] And, as always, it was the armed struggle waged by the Vietnamese themselves – without the pretense of systematic support from the American pacifists – which finally forced the war to a close.[106]

It is evident even from this brief exposition of fact versus fantasy – and the analysis could be extended to much greater length with the same results – that a certain consistency is involved. As with earlier-developed mythologies concerning Gandhi and King (i.e., that their accomplishments were achieved through application of nonviolent principles alone), the current pacifist propaganda line concerning the Vietnam war reveals a truly remarkable propensity to lay claim to progress attained only through the most bitter forms of armed struggle undertaken by others (all the while blandly insisting that the "resort to violence" was/is "inappropriate" to the context of North America).[107]

This already-noted cynical mindwarp holds little appeal to those residing outside the socioeconomic limits of the American comfort zone, and can hardly be expected to recruit them into adhering to nonviolence. However, this *in itself* explains much about American pacifism's real (perhaps subconscious) agenda and reconciles a range of apparent contradictions in the postures of American pacifist strategists.

The Buck Is Passed

We support the just struggles of the NLF in Vietnam . . .

– David Dellinger, 1969

It is immediately perplexing to confront the fact that many of North America's most outspoken advocates of absolute domestic nonviolence when challenging state power have consistently aligned themselves with the most powerful expressions of armed resistance to the exercise of U.S. power *abroad*. Any roster of pacifist luminaries fitting this description would include not only David Dellinger but Joan Baez, Benjamin Spock, A. J. Muste, Holly Near, Staughton Lynd, and Noam Chomsky as well. The situation is all the more problematic when one considers that these leaders, each in his/her own way, also advocate their followers' perpetual diversion into activities prefiguring the nature of a revolutionary society, the basis for which cannot be reasonably expected to appear through nonviolent tactics alone.[108]

This apparent paradox erodes a line of reasoning that, although it has probably never been precisely formulated within the North American nonviolent movement, seems likely to have informed the thinking of its more astute leadership. Its logical contours can be sketched as follows.

Since at least as early as 1916, the importance of

colonial and later neocolonial exploitation of the nonindustrialized world in maintaining modern capitalist states has been increasingly well understood by the revolutionary opposition within those states.[109] Today, it is widely held that removal of neocolonial sources of material and super profits would irrevocably undercut the viability of late capitalist states.[110]

Beginning in the late 1940s with the emergence of both decolonization mandates in international law[111] and the proliferation of armed liberation movements throughout what became known as the "Third World," it became obvious to the opposition within developed states – of which the U.S. had by then assumed hegemonic status – that precisely such an undercutting removal of profits and raw materials was occurring.[112]

It required/requires no particularly sophisticated analysis to perceive that the imposition of colonial/neocolonial forms of exploitation upon Third World populations entailed/entails a degree of systemic violence sufficient to ensure the permanence of their revolt until it succeeds.[113] Similarly, it was/is understandable that Third World revolution would continue of its own volition *whether or not* it was accompanied by overt revolutionary activity within the "mother countries" (advanced capitalist states).[114]

These understandings are readily coupled with the knowledge that the types of warfare evidenced in decolonization struggles were unlikely, under normal circumstances, to trigger superpower confrontations of the type which would threaten mother country populations (including their internal oppositions).[115] Instead, the existence of armed Third World liberation movements would necessitate a continuing range of (token) concessions by the advanced industrial states to their own populations as a means of securing the internal security required for the permanent prosecution of "brush fire wars."[116]

It follows that it is possible for the resident opposition to the advanced industrial states to rely upon the armed efforts of those in the colonies to diminish the relative power of the "mutual enemy," all the while awaiting the "right moment" to take up arms themselves, "completing the world revolution" by bringing down the state. The question then becomes one of when to "seize the time," and who – precisely – it is who will be responsible for "picking up the gun" within the mother country itself.[117]

From here it is possible to extrapolate that when state power has been sufficiently weakened by the liberation struggles of those in the colonies (read: nonwhites), the most oppressed sectors of the mother country population itself (again read nonwhites, often and accurately described as constituting internal colonies) – which are guided by motivations similar to those in the Third World – will be in a position to wage successful armed struggles from within.[118] Such dissolution of the state will mark the ushering in of the postrevolutionary era.

It is possible then to visualize a world revolutionary process in which the necessity of armed participation (and attendant physical suffering) by white radicals is marginalized or dispensed with altogether. Their role in this scenario becomes that of utilizing their already attained economic and social advantages to prefigure, both intellectually and more literally, the shape of the good life to be shared by all in the postrevolutionary context; it is presumed that they will become a (perhaps *the*) crucial social element, having used the "space" (comfort zone) achieved through state concessions generated by the armed pressure exerted by others to the "constructive rather than destructive purpose" of developing a "superior" model of societal relations.[119]

The function of "responsible" oppositional leadership in the mother country – as opposed to the "irresponsible" variety that might precipitate some measure of armed resistance from within before the Third World has bled itself in diminishing state power from without (and who might even go so far as to suggest whites could directly participate) – is first and foremost to link the mother country movement's inaction *symbolically and rhetorically* to Third World liberation struggles. The blatant accommodation to state power involved in this is rationalized (both to the Third Worlders *and* to the movement rank-and-file) by professions of personal and principled pacifism, as well as in the need for "working models" of nonviolent behavior in postrevolutionary society.[120]

From there, the nonviolent American movement (by now overwhelmingly composed of white "progressives") can be steered into exactly the same symbolic and rhetorical "solidarity" with an emerging nonwhite armed revolution within the United States and – voila! – positive social transformation has not only been painlessly achieved (for whites), but they (being the prefigurative nonviolent "experts" on building postrevolutionary society) have maneuvered themselves into leading roles in the aftermath.[121]

All of this, of course, is predicated on the assumption that the colonized, both within and without, will ultimately prove equal to their part, and that revolutionary transformation will actually occur. In the event that the colonizing state ultimately proves the stronger of parties in such a contest, the nonviolent movement – having restricted its concrete activities to limits sanctioned by that same state – will have a natural fall-back position, being as it were only a variant of "the loyal opposition."[122] The result of the carefully-constructed balance (between professed solidarity with armed Third World insurgents on the one hand, and tacit accommodation to the very state power against which they fight on the other) is that North American adherents to nonviolence are intended to win regardless of the outcome; the comfort zone of "white skin privilege" is to be continued in either event. [123]

Or this is the outcome that fence-sitting is expected to accomplish. The range of tremendous ethical, moral, and political problems inherent in this attitude are mostly so self-evident as to require no further explanation or

consideration here. Before turning to the purely pathological characteristics associated with such monumental
(attempted) buck-passing, there is one other primarily
political potentiality which bears at least passing discussion. It is a possibility typically omitted or ignored within
discussions of "the praxis of nonviolence" in the United
States, largely because its very existence would tend to
render pacifism's pleasant (to its beneficiaries) prospec-
tus rather less rosy (read: less appealing to its intended
mass of subscribers). Undoubtedly, the oversight is also
bound up in pacifism's earlier-mentioned arrogance in
presuming it holds some power of superior morality to
determine that the nonviolence of its relations to the state
will necessarily be reciprocated (even to a relative degree)
in the state's relations with pacifists.[124] Whatever the basis for generalized silence in this regard, due consideration must be given to the likelihood that the state, at
some point along its anticipated trajectory of strategic
losses in the hinterlands, will experience the need to re-
constitute its credibility internally, to bring about the
psychic consolidation of its faithful ("morale building"
on the grand scale) by means of a "cleansing of national
life" from within.

Such a transition from liberalistic and cooptive
policies to much more overtly reactionary forms is certainly not without precedent when states perceive their
international power positions eroding, or simply undergoing substantial external threat.[125] Invariably, such circumstances entail the identification (i.e., manufacture),

targeting, and elimination of some internal entity as the "subversive" element undercutting the "national will" and purpose. At such times the state needs no, indeed can tolerate no hint of, domestic opposition; those who are "tainted" by a history of even the milder forms of "anti-social" behavior can be assured of being selected as the scapegoats required for this fascist sort of consensus building.[126]

While the precise form which might be assumed by the scapegoating involved in a consolidation of North American fascism remains unknown, it *is* clear that the posture of the mass nonviolent movement closely approximates that of the Jews in Germany during the 1930s. The notion that "it can't happen here" is merely a parallel to the Jewish perception that it wouldn't happen *there*; insistence on inhabiting a comfort zone even while thousands upon thousands of Third World peasants are cremated beneath canisters of American napalm is only a manifestation of "the attitude of going on with business as usual, even in a holocaust."[127] Ultimately, as Bettelheim observed, it is the dynamic of attempting to restrict opposition to state terror to symbolic and nonviolent responses which gives the state "the idea that [its victims can] be gotten to the point where they [will] walk into the gas chambers on their own."[128] And, as the Jewish experience has shown for anyone who cares to look the matter in the face, the very inertia of pacifist principles prevents any effective conversion to armed self-defense once adherents are targeted for systematic elimination by the state.

Profile of a Pathology

*I just came home from Vietnam where I spent
twelve months of my life trying to pacify the
population. We couldn't do it; their resistance
was amazing. And it was wrong; the process
made me sick. So I came home to join the
resistance in my own country, and I find you
guys have pacified yourselves. That too amazes
me; that too makes me sick . . .*

— Vietnam Veteran Against the War, 1970

A number of logical contradictions and fundamental
misunderstandings of political reality present themselves
within the doctrinal corpus of American pacifist premises
and practices (both as concerns real pacifism and relative
to the modern American "comfort zone" variety).
Matters of this sort are usually remediable, at least to a
significant extent, through processes of philosophical/
political dialogue, factual correction, and the like.[129] Subscribers to the notion of pacifism, however, have proven
themselves so resistant as to be immune to conventional
critique and suasion, hunkering down instead behind a
wall of "principles," *especially* when these can be demonstrated to be lacking both logically and practically in terms
of validity, viability, and utility.[130]

The "blind faith" obstinacy inherent in this position is thus not immediately open to pragmatic, or even

empirical, consideration. It might be more properly categorized within the sphere of theological inquiry (particularly as regards the fundamentalist and occult religious doctrines) – and, indeed, many variants of pacifist dogma acknowledge strong links to an array of sects and denominations – were it not that pacifism asserts itself (generically) not only as a functional aspect of "the real world," but as a praxis capable of engendering revolutionary social transformation.[131] Its basic irrationalities must therefore be taken, on their face, as seriously intended to supplant reality itself.

Codification of essentially religious symbology and mythology as the basis for political ideology (or the psuedoideology *Weltanschauung*) is not lacking in precedent and has been effectively analyzed elsewhere.[132] Although a number of interesting aspects present themselves in the study of any specific fusion of spiritualist impetus with political articulation/practice, the common factor from one example to the next is a central belief that objective conditions (i.e., reality) can be altered by an act of "will" (individual or collective). This is often accompanied by extremely antisocial characteristics, manifested either consciously or subconsciously.[133] The political expression of pacifism confronts us with what may be analogously described as a (mass) pathology.

As with any pathology, pacifism may be said to exhibit a characteristic symptomology by which it can be diagnosed. Salient examples of the complex of factors making up the pathology may be described as follows:

Pacifism is delusional. This symptom is marked by a range of indicators, for example, insistence that reform or adjustment of given state policies constitutes a "revolutionary agenda," insistence that holding candlelight vigils and walking down the street constitute "acts of solidarity" with those engaged in armed struggle, or – despite facts to the contrary – that such things as "the nonviolent decolonization of India" or "the antiwar movement's forcing the Vietnam war to end" actually occurred.

At another level – and again despite clear facts to the contrary – insisting that certain tactics avoid "provoking violence" (when it is already massive) or that by remaining nonviolent pacifism can "morally compel" the state to respond in kind must be considered as deep-seated and persistent delusions.[134]

Finally, it must be pointed out that many supposed "deeply principled" adherents are systematically deluding themselves that they are really pacifists at all. This facet of the symptoms is marked by a consistent avoidance of personal physical risk, an overweaning attitude of personal superiority *vis-à-vis* those who "fail" to make overt professions of nonviolence, and sporadic lapses into rather unpacifist modes of conduct in interpersonal contexts (as opposed to relations with the state).[135]

Pacifism is racist. In displacing massive state violence onto people of colour both outside and inside the mother country, rather than absorbing any real measure of it themselves (even when their physical intervention might undercut the state's ability to inflict violence on nonwhites), pacifists can only be viewed as being objectively racist.

Racism itself has been accurately defined as a pathology.[136] Within the context of pacifism, the basic strain must be considered as complicated by an extremely convoluted process of victim-blaming under the guise of "antiracism" (a matter linking back to the above-mentioned delusional characteristics of the pathology of pacifism).

Finally, both displacement of violence and victim-blaming intertwine in their establishment of a comfort zone for whites who utilize it (perhaps entirely subconsciously) as a basis for "prefiguring" a complex of future "revolutionary" social relations which could serve to largely replicate the present privileged social position of whites, *vis-à-vis* nonwhites, as a cultural/intellectual "élite."[137]

The cluster of subparts encompassed by this overall aspect of the pacifist pathology is usually marked by a pronounced tendency on the part of those suffering the illness to react emotionally and with considerable defensiveness to any discussion (in some cases, mere mention) of the nature of racist behaviors. The behavior is typically manifested in agitated assertions – usually with no accusatory finger having been pointed – to the effect that "I have nothing to be ashamed of" or "I have no reason to feel guilty." As with any pathology, this is the proverbial telltale clue indicating s/he is subliminally aware that s/he has much to be ashamed of and is experiencing considerable guilt as a result. Such avoidance may, in extreme cases, merge once again with delusional characteristics of the pathology.[138]

Pacifism is suicidal. In its core impulse to prostrate itself before the obvious reality of the violence inherent in state power, pacifism not only inverts Emiliano Zapata's famous dictum that "It is better to die on one's feet than to live on one's knees"; it actually posits the proposition that is it *best* to die on one's knees and seeks to achieve this result as a matter of *principle*. Pacifist *Eros* is thus transmuted into *Thanatos*.[139]

While it seems certain that at least a portion of pacifism's propensity toward suicide is born of the earlier-mentioned delusion that it can impel nonviolence on the part of the state (and is therefore simply erroneous), there is a likelihood that one of two other factors is at work in many cases:

1. A sublimated death wish manifesting itself in a rather commonly remarked "gambler's neurosis" (i.e., "Can I risk everything and win?").

2. A desublimated death wish manifesting itself in a "political" equivalent of walking out in front of a bus ("Will it hit me or not?").

In any event, this suicidal pathology may be assumed to follow the contours of other such impulses, centering on repressed guilt neuroses and associated feelings of personal inadequacy (in all probability linked to the above-mentioned subliminal racism) and severely complicated by a delusional insistence that the death wish itself constitutes a "pro-life" impetus. It is interesting to note that the latter claim has been advanced relative to European Jews during the 1940s.[140]

From even this scanty profile, it is easy enough to discern that pacifism – far from being a praxis adequate to impel revolutionary change – assumes the configuration of a pathological illness when advanced as a political methodology. Given its deep-seated, superficially self-serving, and socially approved nature, it is likely to be an exceedingly difficult pathology to treat and a long term barrier to the formation of revolutionary consciousness/action in the North America. Yet it is a barrier which must be overcome if revolutionary change is to occur, and for this reason, we turn to the questions of the nature of the role of nonviolent political action within a viable American transformative praxis, as well as preliminary formulation of a therapeutic approach to the pathology of pacifism.

Toward a Liberatory Praxis

The variegated canvas of the world is before me; I stand over and against it; by my theoretical attitude to it I overcome its opposition to me and make its contents my own. I am at home in the world when I know it, still more so when I have understood it.

— G.W.F. Hegel

While standard definitions tend to restrict the meaning of the term "praxis" to being more or less a sophisticated substitute for the words "action" or "practice," within the tradition of revolutionary theory it yields a more precise quality.[141] August von Cieszkowski long ago observed, "Practical philosophy, or more exactly stated, the Philosophy of Praxis, which could influence life and social relationships, the development of truth in concrete activity – this is the overriding destiny of philosophy."[142] For Marx, the essence of praxis lay in the prospect that the ongoing process of changing circumstances (i.e., material conditions) could coincide with a human self-consciousness which he described as rationally conceived "self-changing" or "revolutionary praxis."[143] In a dialectical sense, this entailed a process of qualitative transformation at the level of totality, from practice (relatively unconscious world-making activity) to praxis (less determined, more conscious world-constituting activity); the distinction between practice and praxis Marx defined as being between something "in-itself" and something "for-itself."[144]

Thus, as Richard Kilminster has noted, for Marx:

The famous 'cunning of Reason' in Hegel's *The Philosophy of History*[145] 'sets of passions' of individuals and the collective aspirations of nations 'to work for itself' in the process of historical self-realization of what it essentially is, as comprehended and exemplified by Reason at its later stages. Strong teleological overtones are present in this conception as they are also in what we might analogously term Marx's implicit notion of a cunning of praxis, through which he discerned history had a consciously appropriable meaning in the blindly developing but ultimately self-rationalizing development of its successive social structures.[146]

In other words, praxis might be accurately defined as action consciously and intentionally guided by theory while simultaneously guiding the evolution of theoretical elaboration. It follows that any liberatory transformation of society is dependent upon the development/articulation of an adequate praxis by which revolutionary struggle may be carried out.[147]

There are a vast range of implications to the praxical symbiosis of theory and practice in prerevolutionary society, most especially within an advanced capitalist context such as that of the United States. To a significant extent, these implications are intellectual/analytical in nature, and the great weight of praxical consideration has correspondingly focused itself in this direction. Insofar as such concerns might rightly be viewed as "strategic," this emphasis is undoubtedly necessary. This is not to say, however, that such preoccupations should be allowed to assume an exclusivist dominance over other matters of legitimate praxical interest. In this regard, the short shrift afforded the more pragmatic or "tactical" aspects of praxis in contemporary dissident theory is, to say the least, disturbing.[148] Such uneven development of praxis is extremely problematic in terms of actualizing revolutionary potential.

A clear example of this tendency may be found in the paucity of recent literature attempting to explore the appropriate *physical* relationship between the repressive/defensive forces of the late capitalist state on the one hand, and those avowedly pursuing its liberatory transformation on the other. Little intellectual or practical effort has gone into examining the precise nature of revolutionary (as opposed to ritual) confrontation or the literal requirements of revolutionary struggle within fully industrialized nations. Consequently, a theoretical – hence, praxical – vacuum has appeared in this connection. And, as with any vacuum of this sort, the analytical default has been filled with the most convenient and readily accessible set of operant assumptions available, in this case with pacifism, the doctrine of "revolutionary nonviolence."

Predictably (for reasons already elaborated), the same situation does not prevail with regard to liberatory struggles in the Third World. In terms of both historiography and mythology, it is considered axiomatic that revolution in nonindustrialized areas all but *inherently* entails resort to armed struggle and violence.[149] This remains true whether one is considering the Bolshevik revolution, the Chinese revolution, the Vietnamese revolution, the Cuban revolution, the Algerian revolution, decolonization struggles in Africa during the 1950s, the

Nicaraguan revolution, the Zimbabwean revolution, or any other.[150] The same principle also holds with regard to Third World liberation movements such as the ANC in South Africa, SWAPO in Namibia, the Tupamaros in Uruguay, the Prestes Column in Brazil, Shining Path in Peru, and so on.[151] In each case, the fundamental physical relationship between armed struggle/violence and liberatory posture is clear.

As a matter of praxis, this relationship has been clarified (even codified) by theorists as diverse as Frantz Fanon, Che Guevara, Mao Tsetung, and Vo Nguyen Giap, to name but a few.[152] The accuracy of their articulations is so compelling that even such a devout (and principled) North American pacifist as Blase Bonpane has observed that, in the Third World, armed struggle is required because "passivity can coexist nicely with repression, injustice, and fascism."[153] Bonpane goes on:

> Unfortunately, we have been brought up on parlor games, where the participants discuss whether or not they are "for" or "against" violence. Can you picture a similar discussion on whether we are for or against disease? Violence, class struggle, and disease are all real. They do not go away through mystification . . . those who deny the reality of violence and class struggle – like those who deny the reality of disease – are not dealing with the real world.[154]

The "real world" of Third World liberatory praxis thus *necessarily* incorporates revolutionary violence as an

integral element of itself. The principle is also extended
to cover certain situations within the less industrialized
sectors of the "First World," as is clearly the situation
relative to the Spanish Civil War, Irish resistance to British colonial rule, resistance to the Greek Junta during the
'60s and '70s, and – to a certain extent at least – within
the context of revolutionary struggle in Italy.[155] Hence,
only within the most advanced – and privileged – sectors of industrial society is armed struggle/violence consigned to the "praxical" realm of "counterproductivity,"
as when the pacifist left queues up to condemn the Black
Panther Party, Weatherman, the Baader-Meinhoff Group,
or its offshoot, the Red Army Faction.[156]

Aside from the obvious moral hypocrisy implicit
in this contradiction, the question must be posed as to
whether it offers any particular revolutionary advantage
to those espousing it. Given the availability of self-pre-
serving physical force in the hands of the state, within
advanced capitalist contexts no less – or even more – than
in colonial/neocolonial situations, the question presents
itself "at the bottom line" as an essentially military one.

Within this analytical paradigm, three cardinal tenets and an axiom must be observed. The tenets are: (1)
the Napoleonic credo that "victory goes to the side field-
ing the biggest battalions" (i.e., those exercising the most
muscle tend to win contests of force); (2) that sheer scale
of force can often be offset through utilization of the element of surprise; and (3) even more than surprise, tactical flexibility (i.e., concentration of force at weak points)

can often compensate for lack of strength or numbers (this is a prime point of ju jitsu). The axiom at issue has been adopted as the motto of the British Special Air Service: "Who dares, wins."[157]

The first tenet is, to be sure, a hopeless proposition at the outset of virtually any revolutionary struggle. The "big battalions" – and balance of physical power – inevitably rest with the state's police, paramilitary, and military apparatus, at least through the initial and intermediate stages of the liberatory process. Consequently, Third World revolutionary tacticians have compensated by emphasizing tenets two and three (surprise and flexibility), developing the art of guerrilla warfare to a very high degree.[158] Within the more industrialized contexts of Europe and North America, this has assumed forms typically referred to as "terrorism."[159] In either event, the method has proven increasingly successful in befuddling more orthodox military thinking throughout the twentieth century, has led to a familiar series of fallen dictators and dismantled colonial regimes, and has substantially borne out the thrust of the "dare to struggle, dare to win" axiom.[160]

The hegemony of pacifist activity and thought within the late capitalist states, on the other hand, not only bows before the balance of power that rests with the status quo in any head-on contest by force, but also gives up the second and third tenets. With activities self-restricted to a relatively narrow band of ritual forms, pacifist tacticians automatically sacrifice much of their (potential) flexibility in confronting the state; within this narrow band, actions become entirely predictable rather than offering the utility of surprise. The bottom-line balance of physical power thus inevitably rests with the state on an essentially permanent basis, and the possibility of liberal social transformation is correspondingly diminished to a point of nonexistence. The British Special Air Force motto is again borne out, this time via a converse formulation: "Who fails to dare, loses . . . perpetually."

It is evident that whatever the attributes of pacifist doctrine, "revolutionary nonviolence" is a complete misnomer, that pacifism itself offers no coherent praxis for liberatory social transformation. At best, it might be said to yield certain aspects of a viable liberatory praxis, thus assuming the status of a sort of "quasi-praxis." More appropriately, it should be viewed more at the level of ideology termed by Louis Althusser as constituting "Generalities I."[161] As a low level of ideological consciousness (i.e., dogma) rather than the manifestation of a truly praxical outlook, pacifism dovetails neatly with Ernest Gellner's observation that ideological "patterns of legitimacy . . . are first and foremost sets of collectively held beliefs about validity. The psychological ground of legitimacy is in fact the recognition of the validity of a given social norm."[162] Or, to take the matter further, we might turn to the conclusion of J. G. Merquoir:

> [A]s far as belief is concerned, ideological legitimacy is chiefly, though not exclusively, for internal consumption. Its function is really to act as a catalyst for the

mind of the group whose interest it sublimates into a justificatory set of ideals. Outside the interest-bound class circle, ideology consists primarily of unchallenged, normally tacit, value-orientations which, once translated into the language of purpose, amounts to the 'manipulation of bias' in favour of privileged groups. (emphasis in original)[163]

This perception of pacifism as a self-justifying ideological preemption of proper praxical consideration, subliminally intended to perpetuate the privileged status of a given "progressive" élite, is helpful in determining what is necessary to arrive at a true liberatory praxis within advanced capitalist contexts. The all but unquestioned legitimacy accruing to the principles of pacifist practice must be continuously and comprehensively subjected to the test of whether they, *in themselves*, are capable of delivering the bottom-line transformation of state-dominated social relations which alone constitutes the revolutionary/liberatory process.[164] Where they are found to be incapable of such delivery, the principles must be broadened or transcended altogether as a means of achieving an adequate praxis.

By this, it is not being suggested that nonviolent forms of struggle are or should be abandoned, nor that armed struggle should be the normative standard of revolutionary performance, either practically or conceptually. Rather, it is to follow the line of thinking recently articulated by Kwame Turé (Stokely Carmichael) when he noted:

If we are to consider ourselves as revolutionaries, we must acknowledge that we have an obligation to succeed in pursuing revolution. Here, we must acknowledge not only the power of our enemies, but our own power as well. Realizing the nature of our power, we must not deny ourselves the exercise of the options available to us; we must utilize surprise, cunning and flexibility; we must use the strength of our enemy to undo him, keeping him confused and off-balance. We must organize with perfect clarity to be utterly unpredictable. When our enemies expect us to respond to provocation with violence, we must react calmly and peacefully; just as they anticipate our passivity, we must throw a grenade. [165]

What is at issue is not therefore the replacement of hegemonic pacifism with some "cult of terror." Instead, it is the realization that, in order to be effective and ultimately successful, any revolutionary movement within advanced capitalist nations must develop the broadest possible range of thinking/action by which to confront the state. This should be conceived not as an array of component forms of struggle but as a continuum of activity stretching from petitions/letter writing and so forth through mass mobilization/demonstrations, onward into the arena of armed self-defense, and still onward through the realm of "offensive" military operations (e.g., elimination of critical state facilities, targeting of key individuals within the governmental/corporate apparatus, etc.). [166] All of this must be apprehended as a holism, as an inter-

nally consistent liberatory process applicable at this gen-
erally-formulated level to the late capitalist context no
less than to the Third World. From the basis of this fundamental understanding – and, it may be asserted, *only*
from this basis – can a viable liberatory praxis for North
America emerge.

It should by now be self-evident that, while a substantial – even preponderant – measure of nonviolent
activity is encompassed within any revolutionary praxis,
there is no place for the profession of "principled pacifism" to preclude – much less condemn – the utilization
of violence as a legitimate and necessary method of achieving liberation.[167] The dismantling of the false consciousness inherent in the ideology of "nonviolent revolution"
is therefore of primary importance in attaining an adequate liberatory praxis.

A Therapeutic Approach to Pacifism

A reversal of perspective is produced vis-à-vis
*adult consciousness: the historical becoming
which prepared it was not before it, it is only
for it; the time during which it progressed is no
longer the time of its constitution, but a time
which it constitutes . . . such is the reply of
critical thought to psychologism, sociologism
and historicism.*

– Maurice Merleau-Ponty, 1947

The pervasiveness of "pacifism" within the ostensibly oppositional sectors of American society appear grounded more in a tightly intertwined complex of pathological characteristics than in some well thought through matrix of consciously held philosophical tenets. To the extent that this is true, the extrapolation of pacifist ideological propositions serves to obfuscate rather than clarify matters of praxical concern, to retard rather than further liberatory revolutionary potentials within the United States. Such a situation lends itself more readily to the emergence of a fascist societal construct than to liberatory transformation.[168] Thus, the need to overcome the hegemony of pacifist thinking is clear.

However, as with any pathologically-based manifestation, hegemonic pacifism in advanced capitalist contexts proves itself supremely resistant – indeed, virtually impervious – to mere logic and moral suasion. The standard accoutrements (such as intelligent theoretical dialogue) of political consciousness raising/movement building have proven relatively useless when confronted within the cynically self-congratulatory obstinacy with which the ideologues of pacifist absolutism defend their faith. What is therefore required as a means of getting beyond the smug exercise of knee-jerk pacifist "superiority," and into the arena of effective liberatory praxis, is a therapeutic rather than dialogic approach to the phenomenon.

What follows, then, is a sketch of a strategy by which radical therapists might begin to work through the pacifist problematic in both individual and group settings.[169] It should be noted that the suggested method of approach is contingent upon the therapist's own freedom from contamination with pacifist predilections (it has been my experience that a number of supposed radical therapists are themselves in acute need of therapy in this area).[170] It should also be noted that, in the process of elaboration, a number of terms from present psychological jargon (e.g., "reality therapy") are simply appropriated for their use value rather than through any formal adherence to the precepts which led to their initial currency. Such instances should be self-explanatory.

Therapy may be perceived as progressing either through a series of related and overlapping stages or phases of indeterminate length.

Values Clarification. During this initial portion of the therapeutic process, participants will be led through discussion/consideration of the bases of need for revolutionary social transformation, both objective and subjective. Differentiations between objectively observed and subjectively felt/experienced needs will be examined in depth, with particular attention paid to contradictions – real or perceived – between the two. The outcome of this portion of the process is to assist each participant in arriving at a realistic determination of whether s/he truly holds values consistent with revolutionary aspirations, or whether s/he is not more psychically inclined toward some variant of reforming/modifying the *status quo*.

The role of the therapist in this setting is to be both extremely conversant with objective factors, and to lead subjective responses of participants to an honest correlation in each discursive moment of process. Although this portion of therapy is quite hypothetical/theoretical in nature, it must be anticipated that a significant portion of participants who began defining themselves as pacifists will ultimately adopt a clarified set of personal values of a nonrevolutionary type, that is, acknowledging that they personally wish to pursue a course of action leading to some outcome other than the total transformation of the state/liberation of the most objectively oppressed social sectors.

It would be possible at this point to posit a procedure for attempting the alteration of nonrevolutionary values. However, the purpose of a radical (as opposed to bourgeois) therapy is not to induce accommodation to principles and values other than their own. In the sense that the term is used here, "values clarification" is merely an expedient to calling things by their right names and to strip away superficial/rhetorical layers of delusion.

Reality Therapy. Those – including self-defined pacifists – who in the initial phase of the process have coherently articulated their self-concept as being revolutionary will be led into a concrete integration with the physical reality of the objective bases for revolution, as well as application(s) of the revolutionary response to these conditions. This phase is quite multifaceted and contains a broad range of optional approaches.

In short, this second phase of the therapeutic process will include direct and extended exposure to the conditions of life among at least one (and preferably more) of the most objectively oppressed communities in North America, for example, inner-city black ghettos, Mexican and Puerto Rican barrios, American Indian reservations or urban enclaves, southern rural black communities, and so on. It is expected that participants will not merely "visit," but remain in these communities for extended periods, eating the food, living in comparable facilities and getting by on the average annual income. Arguments that such an undertaking is unreasonable because it would be dangerous and participants would be unwanted in such communities are not credible; these are the most fundamental reasons *for* going – the reality of existing in perpetual physical jeopardy (and/or of being physically abused in an extreme fashion) precisely *because* of being unwanted (especially on racial grounds), while living in the most squalid of conditions, is precisely what must be understood by self-proclaimed revolutionaries, pacifist or otherwise. Avoiding direct encounters with these circumstances as well as knowledge of them is to avoid revolutionary reality in favor of the comfort zone.

This experience should be followed by a similar sort of exposure to conditions among the oppressed within one or more of the many Third World nations undergoing revolutionary struggle. When at all possible, a part of this process should include linking up directly with one or more of the revolutionary groups operating in that country, a matter which is likely to take time and be dangerous (as will, say, living in an Indian village in Guatemala or Peru). But, again, this is precisely the point; the participant will obtain a clear knowledge of the realities of state repression and armed resistance which cannot be gained in any way other than through direct exposure.

Finally, either during or after the above processes, each participant should engage in some direct and consciously risk-inducing confrontation with state power. This can be done in a myriad of ways, either individually or in a group, but cannot include prior arrangements with police in order to minimize their involvement. Nor can it include obedience to police department demands for "order" once the action begins; participants must adopt a posture of absolute noncooperation with the state while remaining true to their own declared values (e.g., for pacifists, refraining from violent acts themselves).

The role of the therapist – who should already have such grounding in revolutionary reality him/herself – during this phase of therapy is to facilitate the discussion of the process in both individual and group settings. The therapist must be conversant with the realities being experienced by participants to be able to assist them in establishing and apprehending a proper context in each instance.

Evaluation. For those who complete phase two (and a substantial degree of attrition must be anticipated in association with reality therapy, especially among those who began by espousing nonviolent "alternatives" to armed struggle), there must come a period of independent and guided reflection upon their observations and experiences "in the real world." This can be done on a purely individual basis, but generally speaking, a group setting is best for the guided portion of evaluation. A certain recapitulation/reformulation of the outcomes of the values clarification phase is in order, as is considerable philosophical/situational discussion and analysis coupled to readings; role-play has proven quite effective in many instances.

The point of this portion of the therapeutic process is to achieve a preliminary reconciliation of personal, subjective values with concrete realities. A tangible outcome is obtainable in each participant's formal articulation of precisely how he/she sees his/her values coinciding with the demonstrable physical requirements of revolutionary social action. Again, it should be anticipated that during evaluation a segment of participants will arrive at the autonomous decision that their aspirations/commitments are to something other than revolutionary social transformation.

The role of the therapist during this phase is to serve as a consultant to participant self-evaluation, recommend readings as appropriate to participant concerns/confusions, facilitate role-play and other group dynamics, and assist participants in keeping their reconciliations free of contradictions in logic.

Demystification. It has been my experience that, by this point in the therapeutic process, there are few (if any) remaining participants seeking to extend the principles of pacifist absolutism. And among remaining partici-

pants – especially among those who began with such ab-
solutist notions – there often remains a profound lack of
practical insight into the technologies and techniques
common to both physical repression and physical resistance.

A typical psychological manifestation of such ignorance is the mystification of both the tools at issue and
those individuals known to be skilled in their use. For
example, a "fear of guns" is intrinsic to the pacifist left,
as is sheer irrational terror at the very idea of directly
confronting such mythologized characters as members
of SWAT teams, Special Forces ("Green Berets"), Rang-
ers, and members of right-wing vigilante organizations.
The outcomes of such mystification tend to congeal into
feelings of helplessness and inadequacy, rationalization,
and avoidance. Sublimated, these feelings reemerge in
the form of compensatory rhetoric, attempting to con-
vert low self-confidence into a signification of transcend-
ent virtue (i.e., "make the world go away").

Hence, while few participants will at this juncture
be prepared to honestly deny that armed struggle is and
must be an integral aspect of the revolutionary interest
which they profess to share, a number will still contend
that they are "philosophically" unable to directly participate in it. Clarification is obtainable in this connection
by bringing out the obvious: knowing how, at some
practical level, to engage in armed struggle and then
choosing not to is a much different proposition than
refraining from such engagement due to ignorance of the

means and methods involved.

Here, "hands-on" training and experience is of the essence. The basic technologies at issue – rifles, assault rifles, handguns, shotguns, explosives, and the like, as well as the rudiments of their proper application and deployment – must be explored. This practical training sequence should be augmented and enhanced by selected readings, and continual individual and group discussions of the meaning(s) of this new range of skills acquisition.[171]

It should be noted clearly that this phase of therapy is *not* designed or intended to create "commandos" or to form guerrilla units. Rather, it will serve only to acquaint each participant with the fact that s/he has the same general information/skills base as those who deter him/her through physical intimidation or repression and is at least potentially capable of the same degree of proficiency in these formerly esoteric areas as their most "élite" opponents. At this point, nonviolence *can* become a philosophical choice or tactical expedient rather than a necessity born of psychological default.

The role of the therapist during this phase is unlikely to be that of trainer (although it is possible, given that he/she should have already undergone such training). Rather, it is likely to be that of suggesting the appropriate trainers and literature, and serving as discussion/group facilitator for participants.

Reevaluation. In this final phase of therapy, remaining participants will be led into articulation of their overall perspective on the nature and process of revolutionary social transformation (i.e., their understanding of liberatory praxis), including their individual perceptions of their own specific roles within this process. The role of the therapist is to draw each participant out into a full and noncontradictory elaboration, as well as to facilitate the emergence of a potential for future, ongoing reevaluation and development of revolutionary consciousness.

The internal composition of each phase of this therapeutic approach in resolving the problem of hegemonic (pathological) pacifism is open to almost infinite variation on the part of the therapists and participants involved in each instance of application. Even the ordering of phases may be beneficially altered; for example, what has been termed "reality therapy" may have independently preceded and triggered the perceived need for values clarification on the part of some (or many) participants. Or, independently undertaken evaluations may lead some participants to enter values clarification and then proceed to reality therapy. The key for therapists is to retain a sense of flexibility of approach when applying the model, picking up participants at their own points of entry and adapting the model accordingly, rather than attempting some more-or-less rigid progression.

In sum, it is suggested that the appropriate application of the broad therapeutic model described in this section can have the effect of radically diminishing much of the delusion, the aroma of racism and the sense of privilege which mark the covert self-defeatism accompanying the practice of mainstream dissident politics in contemporary America. At another level – if widely adopted – the model will be of assistance in allowing the construction of a true liberatory praxis, a real "strategy to win," for the first time within advanced industrial society. This potentiality, for those who would claim the mantle of being revolutionary, can only be seen as a positive step.

Conclusion

In the contradiction lies the hope.
— Bertholt Brecht

This essay is far from definitive. Its composition and emphasis have been dictated largely by the nature of the dialogue and debate prevailing within the circle of the American opposition today. The main weight of its exposition has gone to critique pacifist thinking and practice; its thrust has been more to debunk the principles of hegemonic nonviolence rather than to posit fully articulated alternatives. In the main, this has been brought about by the degree of resistance customarily thrown up, *a priori*, to any challenge extended to the assumption of ontological goodness pacifism accords itself. The examples it raises are intended to at least give pause to those whose answers have been far too pat and whose "purity of purpose" has gone unquestioned for far too long.

A consequence of this has been that the conceptualization of other options, both within this essay and in the society beyond, have suffered. As concerns society, this is an obviously unacceptable situation. As to the essay, it may be asserted that it is to the good. The author is neither vain nor arrogant enough to hold that his single foray could be sufficient to offset the magnitude of problematic issues raised. Instead, it is to be hoped that the emphasis of "Pacifism as Pathology" will cause sufficient anger and controversy that others – many others – will endeavor to seriously address the matters at hand. Within such open and volatile forums, matters of therapeutic and praxical concerns can hopefully advance.

In concluding, I would at last like to state the essential premise of this essay clearly: the desire for a non-violent and cooperative world is the healthiest of all psychological manifestations. *This* is the overarching principle of liberation and revolution.[172] Undoubtedly, it seems the highest order of contradiction that, in order to achieve nonviolence, we must first break with it in overcoming its root causes. Therein, however, lies our only hope.

Notes

1. On the matter of alchemy, at least as intended here, *see* Louis Pauwels and Jacques Bergier, *The Morning of the Magicians* (New York: Stein and Day, 1964) pp. 62–90.

2. V. I. Lenin, *State and Revolution* (New York: International, 1932).

3. The tally of twentieth-century revolutions accomplished through nonviolent means is exactly zero (*see* the critique of the Gandhian "exception" in the section "An Essential Contradiction").

4. E.g., Committee in Solidarity with the People of El Salvador (CISPES).

5. Probably the best elucidation of the "oppositional praxis" at issue here can be found in Gene Sharp's 902-page trilogy, *The Politics of Nonviolent Action* (Boston: Porter Sargent, 1973), "Part One: Power and Struggle"; "Part Two: The Methods of Nonviolent Action"; and "Part Three: The Dynamic of Nonviolent Action." Meanwhile, on the steady growth of native fascism, *see* Phillip Finch, *God, Guts and Guns: A Close Look at the Radical Right* (New York: Seaview, 1983); James Coates, *Armed and Dangerous: The Rise of the Survivalist Right* (New York: Noonday, 1987); and Russ Bellant, *Old Nazis, the New Right, and the Republican Party: Domestic Fascist Networks and Their Effect on U.S. Cold War Politics* (Boston: South End Press, 1991).

6. *See*, e.g., Gene Sharp, *Social Power and Political Freedom* (Boston: Porter Sargent, 1980).

7. Virtually all extant literature on the subject, which is considerable, leaves the same impression on this point. William L. Shirer, "The New Order," *The Rise and Fall of the Third Reich: A History of Nazi Germany* (New York: Simon & Schuster, 1960), Chapt. 2, pp. 937–94, still provides as good a capsule view as any single volume.

8. On this point there are also numerous sources. For example, *see* Hannah Arendt, *Eichmann in Jerusalem: A Report on the Banality of Evil* (New York: Penguin Books, 1963), pp. 41–48; Heinz Hohne, *The Order of the Death's Head,* Richard Barry, trans. (New York: Coward McCann, 1970), pp. 346–47; and Helmut Krausnik et al., *Anatomy of the SS State,* Richard Barry et al., trans. (New York: Walker & Co., 1968), pp. 54–57.

9. Raul Hilberg, *The Destruction of the European Jews* (Chicago: Quadrangle, 1961), pp. 122–25, 297, 316.

10. Isaiah Trunk, *Judenrat: The Jewish Councils in Eastern Europe Under Nazi Occupation* (New York: Macmillan, 1972); Raul Hilberg, "The Judenrat: Conscious or Unconscious Tool?," *Proceedings of the Third Vad Yashem International Historical Conference, 4–7 April 1977* (Jerusalem: Yad Vashem, 1979).

11. *See* Primo Levi, *Survival in Auschwitz: The Nazi Assault on Humanity* (New York: Collier Books, 1961); Miklos Nyiszli, *Auschwitz* (New York: Fawcett Books, 1960); and Terrance Des Pres, *The Survivor: Anatomy of Life in the Death Camps* (New York: Oxford University Press, 1980).

12. The most careful recent estimates indicate that approximately 5.1 million Jews perished in the Holocaust, 1.1 million in Auschwitz/ Birkenau alone; Raul Hilberg, *The Destruction of the European Jews*, 3 vols. (New York: Holmes and Meier, rev. ed., 1985), Vol. 3, pp. 1047–48, 1201–20. *See* also, Franciszek Piper, "The Number of Victims," in *Anatomy of the Auschwitz Death Camp*, Yisrael Gutman and Michael Berenbaum, eds. (Bloomington: Indiana University Press, 1994), pp. 61–76.

13. The question is posed in a number of places by various authors. The particular version used here was framed by Bruno Bettelheim on p. ix of his Foreword to Nyiszli, *Auschwitz*, 1960, op. cit.

14. Again, the references on this point are quite numerous. As examples, *see* Hilberg, *The Destruction of European Jews*, op. cit.; Hilberg, Martyrs & Heroes Remembrance Authority, *The Holocaust* (Jerusalem, Palestine: Vad Yashem, 1975); and Irving Louis Horowitz, *Genocide: State Power & Mass Murder* (New Brunswick, New Jersey: Transaction Books, 1976).

15. E.g., Yehuda Bauer, *The Holocaust as Historical Experience: Essays and Discussion* (New York: Holmes and Meir, 1981).

16. But not, as assorted zionist propagandists such as Yehuda Bauer, Deborah Lipstadt, Emil Fackenheim, Lucy Dawidowicz and Steven T. Katz would have it, to a degree unique in all history. Slavs, Gypsies, homosexuals, and leftists shared a similar fate under nazi rule. Approximately two-thirds of Europe's Jews were exterminated by the nazis, while at least the same percentage (and probably more) of all North American Indians were slaughtered by the United States and its colonial antecedents. The butchery of Armenians by Turks in 1915 also rivals the Holocaust in intensity, if not in scale, as does the genocide of East Timorese by Indonesia between 1975 and 1977, and – in some respects – the treatment accorded Palestinians by Israel today. *See* generally, Bohdan Wytwycky, *The Other Holocaust:*

Many Circles of Hell: A Brief Account of the 9–10 Million Persons Who Died with 6 Million Jews Under Nazi Racism (Washington, D.C.: Novac Report on the New Ethnicity, 1980); Frank Chalk and Kurt Jonassohn, *The History and Sociology of Genocide: Analyses and Case Studies* (New Haven: Yale University Press, 1990); Michael Berenbaum, ed., *A Mosaic of Victims: Non-Jews Persecuted and Murdered by the Nazis* (New York: New York University Press, 1990); and Alan S. Rosenbaum, ed., *Is the Holocaust Unique? Perspectives on Comparative Genocide* (Boulder, Colorado: Westview Press, 1996).

  17. Actually, to be fair, such accusations transcend zionism. A classic example occurred during the preparation of this manuscript. It was sent out for review and comments to a Denver-based *anti*-zionist Jewish organization, which was sharply critical of the use of the Holocaust to illustrate many of the points made herein. The very first objection raised was that using "'Like Lambs to the Slaughter' as a heading is just asking to be called anti-semitic, especially since the argument does not reflect the facts." Interestingly, among the materials sent along to "correct" my factual understanding of the extent and effectiveness of Jewish armed resistance to the Holocaust was a xeroxed excerpt from Lucy Dawidowicz's *War Against the Jews, 1933–1945* (New York: Holt, Rinehart & Wilson, 1975) containing the following passage at p. 423: "The only question facing the Jews [announced a zionist leader in 1943] was how to choose to die: 'either like sheep for the slaughter or like men of honor.' Among the Zionist youth in the resistance movement, 'like sheep for the slaughter' became an epithet of ignominy, divorced from its original [Hebraic] meaning of martyrdom. These young Zionists, in their statements and proclamations, [expressed] a feeling of anger against Jewish passivity." I may perhaps be forgiven for observing that this is *exactly* the argument I've been making. One can accept it or reject it, but one cannot do both at once (as my critics seek to do). And, to label as "anti-semitic" the application of an explicitly Jewish term to a context and in a fashion in which it has already been emphatically applied by Jews? Unto me giveth a break. This is not constructive criticism. Rather, it is the use of name-calling and factual distortion to foreclose on inconvenient discussion. One solace is that being subjected to such nonsense places me in some pretty good company; Jewish scholars like Hannah Arendt, Raul Hilberg, and Arno J. Mayer have suffered similar indignities at the hands of their own community after raising comparably uncomfortable issues with respect to the Judaic response to nazism; *see* Dwight Macdonald, "Hannah Arendt and the Jewish Establishment," in

his *Discriminations: Essays and Afterthoughts* (New York: Grossman, 1974); on Hilberg, *see* Michael R. Marrus, "Jewish Resistance to the Holocaust," *Journal of Contemporary History,* No. 30 (1995); and Arno J. Mayer, "History and Memory: On the Poverty of Remembering and Forgetting the Judeocide," *Radical History Review,* No. 56 (1993). For further, and entirely cogent, consideration of the "like sheep to the slaughter" phenomenon and its implications, *see* Robert G. L. Waite, "The Holocaust and Historical Explanation," in *Genocide and the Modern Age: Etiology and Case Studies of Mass Death,* Isidor Wallimann and Michael N. Dobkowski, eds. (Westport, Connecticut: Greenwood Press, 1987).

18. Bettelheim, op. cit., p. xiv.

19. It should be noted that similar revolts in Sobibór and Treblinka in 1943 were even more effective than the one at Auschwitz/Birkenau a few months later; Sobibór had to be closed altogether, a reality which amplifies and reinforces Bettelheim's rather obvious point; Miriam Novitch, *Sobibór: Martyrdom and Revolt* (New York: Holocaust Library, 1980); Jean-François Steiner, *Treblinka* (New York: Simon & Schuster, 1967); and Yisrael Gutman, "Rebellions in the Camps: Three Revolts in the Face of Death," in *Critical Issues of the Holocaust,* Alex Grobman and Daniel Landes, eds. (Los Angeles: Simon Wiesenthal Center, 1983).

20. Bettelheim, op. cit., p. xi.

21. *Ibid.,* p. vi. Similar observations have been made by others, notably Hilberg in the 1985 edition of *The Destruction of the European Jews* (op. cit.); and Arno J. Mayer, in his *Why Did the Heavens Not Darken? The "Final Solution" in History* (New York: Pantheon, 1990), as well as elsewhere.

22. Bettelheim, op. cit., p. viii.

23. A succinct overview of the Nuremberg Laws and related pieces of nazi legislation can be found in Stefan Kühl, *The Nazi Connection: Eugenics, American Racism, and German National Socialism* (New York: Oxford University Press, 1994), pp. 73, 97–98.

24 Bettelheim, op. cit., p. x.

25. *Ibid.*

26. It is apprehension of precisely this point, whether concretely or intuitively, which seems to be guiding a school of revisionism which seeks to supplant images of the passivity of the preponderance of Jews during the Holocaust with a rather distorted impression that armed resistance to nazism was pervasive among this victim group. Probably the definitive effort in this connection is Reuben Ainsztein's massive *Jewish Re-*

sistance in Nazi-Occupied Eastern Europe: With a Historical Survey of the Jew as Fighter and Soldier in the Diaspora (New York: Barnes and Nobel, 1974). Other noteworthy contributions to the literature in this respect include Isaiah Trunk's *Jewish Responses to Nazi Persecution: Collective and Individual Behavior in Extremis* (New York: Stein and Day, 1979); and Yehuda Bauer's "Jewish Resistance and Passivity in the Face of the Holocaust," in *Unanswered Questions: Nazi Germany and the Genocide of the Jews,* François Furet, ed. (New York: Schocken Books, 1989). These efforts, and others like them, perform an admirable service in fleshing out the woefully incomplete record of Jewish resistance – and perhaps to counter notions that Jewish passivity resulted from congenital or cultural "cowardice," misimpressions which should never have held currency anyway – but they do nothing to render the extent of Jewish armed struggle greater than it was. Arguments to the contrary – such as that advanced by the critics mentioned in endnote 17 are purely polemical (or emotional).

27. This "spiritual dimension" has in fact been one of the major thematics of the most noted analysts of the meaning of the Holocaust, Elie Wiesel; *see Confronting the Holocaust: The Impact of Elie Wiesel,* Alvin H. Rosenfeld and Irving Greenberg, eds. (Bloomington: Indiana University Press, 1978).

28. As to the implications of the disarmed and therefore utterly unprepared state of the Jewish resistance in its efforts to formulate an adequate response to the nazis, *see* Bauer, "Resistance and Passivity," op. cit., pp. 240-41.

29. For a taste of such reasoning, *see* David Garrow's Pulitzer Prize winning *Bearing the Cross: Martin Luther King, Jr., and the Southern Christian Leadership Conference* (New York: William Morrow, 1986).

30. This is the premise advanced in works such as Joan Bondurant's *The Conquest of Violence: The Gandhian Philosophy of Conflict* (Berkeley: University of California Press, 1973).

31. Lesser insurrections "took place in Kruszyna, Krychow, and Lublin prisoner-of-war camp, the Kopernik camp at Minsk-Mazowiecki, at Sachsenhausen, and perhaps elsewhere"; Bauer, "Resistance and Passivity," op. cit., p. 243.

32. For an excellent account of the only recorded mass Jewish armed resistance to extermination, *see* Emmanuel Ringlebaum, *Notes from the Warsaw Ghetto: The Journal of Emmanuel Ringlebaum* (New York: McGraw-Hill, 1958). A much smaller ghetto revolt occurred in Bialystok in August 1943. Additionally, there were "three armed revolts [and] four attempted

rebellions" in ghettos in the Polish General Government area during 1942–1943; Bauer, "Resistance and Passivity," op. cit., pp. 241–42.

33. Again, to be fair, it wasn't just the SS, a point made long ago by Gerald Reitlinger in his *The SS: Alibi of a Nation* (New York: Viking, 1957). Aside from this exterminatory élite, large numbers of rather common Germans participated voluntarily and with enthusiasm in the Final Solution; *see* Christopher R. Browning, *Ordinary Men: Reserve Police Battalion 101 and the Final Solution in Poland* (New York: HarperCollins, 1992); and Daniel Jonah Goldhagen, *Hitler's Willing Executioners: Ordinary Germans and the Holocaust* (New York: Alfred A. Knopf, 1996). Indeed, there is substantial evidence that a majority of Germans knew of and to varying extents endorsed the nazi Judeocide; John Weiss, *Ideology of Death: Why the Holocaust Happened in Germany* (Chicago: Ivan R. Dee, 1996).

34. *See* Gerald Fleming, *Hitler and the Final Solution* (Berkeley: University of California Press, 1982); Hohne, op cit.; Hilberg, *The Destruction of European Jews*, op. cit., 1961 edition; and Horowitz, op. cit.

35. *See* generally, Henry L. Feingold, *The Politics of Rescue: The Roosevelt Administration and the Holocaust, 1938–1945* (New Brunswick, New Jersey: Rutgers University Press, 1970).

36. For the best account of the apprehension of Eichmann, *see* Isser Harel, *The House on Garibaldi Street* (New York: Viking, 1975). *See* also Arendt, op. cit.

37. Quoted in Arendt, op. cit., p. 17.

38. Gandhi himself is rather candid about this, as is evidenced in his autobiographical *All Men Are Brothers* (New York: Continuum, 1982).

39. For an adequate assessment of this factor, *see* Alan Campbell-Johnson, *Mission with Montbatten* (London: Robert Hale, 1951), pp. 119-34. *See* also Bondurant, op. cit.

40. Louis Fischer, *The Life of Mahatma Gandhi* (New York: Harpers, 1950), especially Chapt. II; Leo Kuper, *Passive Resistance in South Africa* (New Haven, Connecticut: Yale University Press, 1957). This reality is a bit different from that claimed for the Mahatma by his adherents from very early on; *see*, e.g., Krishnala Shridharani, *War Without Violence: A Study of Gandhi's Method and Its Accomplishments* (New York: Harcourt, Brace, 1939).

41. An excellent summary of the relationship between SNCC and King's main organization, the Southern Christian Leadership Conference, can be found in Howard Zinn, *SNCC: The New Abolitionists* (Boston: Beacon Press, 1967). Further depth is added with regard to the organization's

abandonment of nonviolent principles in Stokely Carmichael and Charles V. Hamilton, *Black Power: The Politics of Liberation in America* (New York: Vintage, 1967), especially p. 97.

42. H. Rap Brown, *Die Nigger Die!* (New York: Dial, 1969) contains a very lucid elaboration of the context of Black Power. *See* also Robert F. Williams, *Negroes with Guns* (Chicago: Third World Press, 1962); Nathan Wright, Jr., *Black Power and Urban Unrest* (New York: Hawthorn, 1967); Julius Lester, *Look Out, Whitey! Black Power's Gon' Get Your Mama* (New York: Dial, 1968).

43. Or most of it, anyway. It is clear that FBI Director J. Edgar Hoover continued to manifest a virulent hatred of King, personally, using the power of his agency in a relentless effort to destroy the civil rights leader; David Garrow, *The FBI and Dr. Martin Luther King, Jr.* (New York: Penguin, 1981). Rather murkier is the possibility that the bureau participated in orchestrating King's 1968 assassination; *see*, e.g., Mark Lane and Dick Gregory, *Code Name "Zorro": The Assassination of Dr. Martin Luther King, Jr.* (Englewood Cliffs, New Jersey: Prentice-Hall, 1977).

44. The rider, attached to the bill by paleoconservative senator Strom Thurmond, made it a federal felony to cross state lines "with intent to incite riot." While enforcement of many of the act's ostensibly affirmative provisions has languished, the rider was immediately applied with vigor in an effort to neutralize what was perceived by authorities as being the leadership of an array of dissident movements; Jason Epstein, *The Great Conspiracy Trial: An Essay on Law, Liberty and the Constitution* (New York: Random House, 1970).

45. Even the title of King's last book, *Where Do We Go From Here: Chaos or Community?* (New York: Bantam, 1967), suggests he was consciously using the existence of an armed or "violent" trend among politicized American blacks as a foil against which to further the objectives of his own nonviolent movement. In other words, without a number of his ostensible constituents "picking up the gun," King was rendered rather less effective in pursuit of his own pacifist politics.

46. It can, of course, be pointed out that the Jews really constituted no threat at all to the nazi state, and that assertions to the contrary (especially genocidal ones) were/are ridiculously irrational. True. However, this does nothing to disrupt the logic or structure of the situation. The fact is that nazi theoreticians and policy makers *perceived* the Jews as a threat, and their programs were formulated accordingly. As Robert Cecil demonstrates compellingly in *The Myth of the Master Race: Alfred Rosenburg and*

Nazi Ideology (New York: Dodd Mead, 1972), the nazis really *did* believe, among other things, in the existence of a "Red (communist), Black (anarchist) and Gold (banker) Conspiracy" of Jews which they were duty-bound to eradicate. The fact that their exercise of state power was completely irrational did nothing to alter the fact of that power, or to save one Jew from the effects of it. Nor is the situation as aberrant as it might first appear; the reader is invited to compare the virulence of nazi antisemitism during the pre-genocidal 1930s to the nature of official U.S. anticommunism especially during the McCarthy era. This is but one parallel.

47. An interesting study in this connection is Mark Calloway's aptly titled *Heavens on Earth: Utopian Communities in America, 1680–1880* (New York: Dover, 1966). It will be observed that each pacifist "prefiguration" of a broader social application proved an abject failure (this is as distinct from the much more sustained – but completely insular – employment of many of the same principles by religious communities such as the Amish).

48. Sharp, *Gandhi as Political Strategist*, op. cit.

49. *See*, e.g., Seth Cagin and Philip Dray, *We Are Not Afraid: The Story of Goodman, Schwerner and Chaney and the Civil Rights Campaign for Mississippi* (New York: Macmillan, 1988).

50. A succinct but comprehensive elaboration of the literal context in which the self-immolations occurred may be found in Michael MacClear, *The Ten Thousand Day War: Vietnam, 1945–1975* (New York: St. Martin's Press, 1981); on the monks, *see* pp. 63–64; for information on Morrison, *see* p. 143. For an assessment of the media context, *see* Todd Gitlin, *The Whole World Is Watching: Mass Media in the Making and Unmaking of the New Left* (Berkeley: University of California Press, 1980).

51. If, as has been plausibly suggested, the monks' real agenda was more to eliminate the Diem regime than American presence per se, their campaign must be assessed as rather more successful than would otherwise be the case. Largely as a result of the furor and negative PR image generated in the United States by the self-immolations and Saigon's utterly callous response, Diem was ousted in a coup d'etat on the night of November 1–2, 1963. It should be noted, however, that the coup was accomplished by the military and in an emphatically violent fashion (Diem and his brother, Nhu, were assassinated), an outcome which is hardly pacifist. *See* Stanley Karnow, *Vietnam: A History* (New York: Penguin, 1984), pp. 206–39.

52. Jack Nelson and Ronald J. Ostrow, *The FBI and the Berrigans: The Making of a Conspiracy* (New York: Coward, McCann & Geoghegan, 1972).

53. This is well-covered in Reed Brody, *Contra Terror in Nicaragua* (Boston: South End Press, 1985).

54. *See*, e.g., Susan Zakin, *Coyotes and Town Dogs: Earth First! and the Environmental Movement* (New York: Viking, 1993); and Judi Bari, *Timber Wars* (Monroe, Maine: Common Courage, 1994).

55. Let's be clear on this point: "revolution" means to obliterate the existing status quo and replace it with something else, *not* to engage in reformist efforts to render it "better" while leaving it in place. Revolution thus implies a fundamental rejection of things as they are; reform implies a fundamental acceptance.

56. For a summary of this trend, *see* David Zane Mairowitz, *The Radical Soap Opera: The Roots of Failure in the American Left* (New York: Avon, 1974).

57. The principles are laid out clearly in Bradford Lyttle's *The Importance of Discipline in Demonstrations for Peace* (New York: Committee for Nonviolent Action, 1962). Abbie Hoffman does a good job of analyzing this phenomenon in his *Revolution for the Hell of It* (New York: Dial, 1968). More broadly, *see* Dana Beal et al., eds., *Blacklisted News: Secret History from Chicago, 1968 to 1984* (New York: Bleecker, 1983.

58. Excellent elaborations concerning police functions can be found in Lynn Cooper, et al., *The Iron First and the Velvet Glove: An Analysis of U.S. Police* (Berkeley: Center for Research on Criminal Justice, 1975); David Wise, *The American Police State: The Government Against the People* (New York: Random House, 1976).

59. At another level, *see* the critique offered by Daniel Cohn-Bendit of the Communist Party's collaboration to the same end with the Gaulist government during the 1968 French student/worker uprising in his *Obsolete Communism: The Left-Wing Alternative* (New York: McGraw-Hill, 1968).

60. *See* Herbert Marcuse, "Repressive Tolerance," in *A Critique of Pure Tolerance,* Robert Paul Wolff, Barrington Moore, Jr., and Herbert Marcuse, eds. (Boston: Beacon Press, 1969), pp. 81–117, especially pp. 101–02.

61. *See* Gitlin, op. cit., Chapt. 7, "Elevating Moderating Alternatives: The Moment of Reform," pp. 205–32.

62. *New Left Notes* (Apr. 1968).

63. For an excellent overall sampling of the more professional efforts at such advertising, *see Images of an Era: The American Poster, 1945–1975* (Washington, D.C.: Smithsonian Institution, 1975). *See* also Mitchell

Goodman, ed., *The Movement Toward a New America: The Beginnings of a Long Revolution* (Philadelphia/New York: Pilgrim/Alfred A. Knopf, 1970).

64. Barbara Epstein, "The Politics of Symbolic Protest," *Redline* (Mar. 1988).

65. What is at issue is an altogether different matter from the identically named training delivered to SNCC volunteers prior to their going "on line" in locales like rural Mississippi in the early '60s. The SNCC training was designed to provide survival skills in the face of the virtual certainty that volunteers would suffer vicious physical assaults from the police while its supposed equivalent in the '80s (and '90s) is predicated on the opposite expectation. On the nature and assumptions of SNCC training, *see* Clayborne Carson, *In Struggle: SNCC and the Black Awakening of the 1960s* (Cambridge: Harvard University Press, 1981). The same general rule applies to the kind of instruction provided by the Revolutionary Youth Movement/Weatherman wing of SDS; Kathy Boudin, et al., *The Bust Book: What to Do Until the Lawyer Comes* (New York: Grove Press, 1969).

66. A prime example is that of the annual protests of nuclear weapons testing in Nevada during the 1980s; this is well covered in Rebecca Solnit's *Savage Dreams: A Journey into the Hidden Wars of the American West* (San Francisco: Sierra Club Books, 1994).

67. E.g., during a carefully orchestrated protest of the annual Columbus Day celebration in 1990, Russell Means, a leader of the American Indian Movement of Colorado, poured a gallon of imitation blood over a statue of the "Great Discoverer" in the city's central plaza (He was thereupon issued a citation for "desecrating a venerated object."). Ultimately, in forcing the cancellation of the Columbus Day event by 1992 – the 500th anniversary of the Columbian landfall – Colorado AIM used every nonviolent tactic mentioned in this section. What separates AIM's stance from that of the entities critiqued in this essay is that its strategy has never foreclosed upon armed struggle. To the contrary, it has consistently employed the latter as and when such methods have seemed appropriate. Hence, its strategic posture evidences the full continuum of tactical options.

68. For a panoramic overview, *see* Barbara Epstein, *Political Protest and Cultural Revolution: Nonviolent Direct Action in the 1970s and 1980s* (Berkeley: University of California Press, 1991).

69. Consider, for example, the perfectly orderly mass arrests of more than 500 individuals protesting CIA recruitment on the University of Colorado's Boulder campus in 1985. No bail was required, and no cases

were prosecuted. Instead, some arrestees were known to frame their "obstruction" citations in the same manner that they might other honors, awards, and diplomas. CIA recruitment, incidentally, continues at the institution more than a decade later.

70. There are, of course, exceptions, as when a group of pacifists from Silo-Plowshares managed to get into a nuclear weapons compound near Chicago during the early '80s and attempted to disable several missiles. The potential efficacy of this technique – as opposed to holding "vigils" outside the facility's gates – caused the government to make "deterrent examples" of the "culprits." The offending Plowshares activists were promptly labeled as "terrorists" – a matter which shows clearly that political effectiveness rather than use of violence is the defining characteristic underlying official use of the term – and two of them were subsequently incarcerated in the federal "super-maximum" prison at Marion, Illinois, for several years. So outrageous was the government's distortion of the facts in this case that at least one veteran FBI agent, John Ryan, resigned rather than participate in the frame-up; "Once a G-Man, Now a Pacifist: A Costly Conversion," *Newsweek* (23 Nov. 1987).

71. Again, there are always exceptions (which, of course, simply prove the rule). The Plowshares case mentioned in the preceding note is salient. The leadership of the AIM protests mentioned in note 67 were prosecuted with the intent that they suffer a year's imprisonment. For another good illustration, *see* Daniel Berrigan, *The Trial of the Catonsville Nine* (Boston: Beacon Press, 1970).

72. Former U.S. Defense Secretary Robert S. McNamara, in an interview on *Larry King Live* (May 1996), placed the overall tally of Indochinese corpses at 3.2 million; On Chile, *see* Jorge Palacios, *Chile: An Attempt at "Historic Compromise"* (Chicago: Banner, 1979). On El Salvador, *see* Maria Teresa Tula, *Hear My Testimony* (Boston: South End Press, 1994). On Guatemala, *see* Edward R. F. Sheehan, *Agony in the Garden: A Stranger in Guatemala* (New York: Houghton-Mifflin, 1989). On Grenada, *see* Edwin P. Hoyt, *America's Wars and Military Incursions* (New York: McGraw-Hill, 1987), pp. 531-45. On Panama, *see* the Independent Commission of Inquiry on the U.S. Invasion of Panama, *The U.S. Invasion of Panama: The Truth Behind Operation "Just Cause"* (Boston: South End Press, 1991). On Nicaragua, *see* Holly Sklar, *Washington's War on Nicaragua* (Boston: South End Press, 1989). On the Gulf war, *see* Cynthia Peters, ed., *Collateral Damage* (Boston: South End Press, 1992).

73. For a comprehensive study of such "overlooked" matters as the

U.S.-supported Indonesian genocide in East Timor, circa 1975–1977, *see* Noam Chomsky and Edward S. Herman, *The Political Economy of Human Rights,* Vols. I & II (Boston: South End Press, 1979). *See* also A. J. Langguth, *Hidden Terrors: The Truth About U.S. Police Operations in Latin America* (New York: Pantheon Books, 1978), for an in-depth examination of such things on a hemispheric basis. William Blüm's *Killing Hope: U.S. Military and CIA Interventions Since World War II* (Monroe, Maine: Common Courage, 1995) will round out the picture through the end of the 1980s. Daniel P. Bolger's *Savage Peace: Americans at War in the 1990s* (San Francisco: Presidio, 1995) will help fill in gaps for the early '90s.

74. In her autobiography, *Growing Up Underground* (New York: William Morrow, 1981), Jane Alpert offers vivid recollections of her fear that nonviolent "allies" would turn her in to the police should her identity as a fugitive bomber of corporate targets become known to them. Her "paranoia" was justified by the probability that Weather fugitives such as Cathy Wilkerson had already been apprehended on the basis of tips to the police provided by pacifists with "principled objections to the Weatherman's political violence." For an amazingly candid (if unintended) profession of support for the police *vis-à-vis* armed oppositional cadres by a "pacifist feminist," *see* Ellen Frankfort, *Kathy Boudin and the Dance of Death* (New York: Stein and Day, 1983); that Frankfort's incredibly racist and reactionary views are widely shared, at least among pacifist feminists, is evidenced by the excellent reviews her book received. The whole squalid trend probably culminated with the publication of Robin Morgan's *The Demon Lover: On the Sexuality of Terrorism* (New York: W. W. Norton, 1989).

75. David Dellinger, "The Bread is Rising," in *Beyond Survival: New Directions for the Disarmament Movement,* Michael Albert and David Dellinger, eds. (Boston: South End Press, 1983), p. 33. One is at a loss as to what to make of such a statement. How does he know such a program would be counterproductive, given support rather than obstruction by people like him? Such a context, after all, has never been evident in the United States. Further, Dellinger has often been quite vocal in his support for armed struggle *elsewhere* (e.g., the National Liberation Front in Vietnam). Could it be that he perceives resort to arms to be more viable when other than *American* activists will do the fighting? For further insight, *see* Dellinger's *Vietnam Revisited: Covert Action to Invasion to Reconstruction* (Boston: South End Press, 1986).

76. Sam Brown, "Statement to the Associated Press" (5 Dec. 1969).

It is perhaps indicative of Brown's notion of the importance of symbolic rather than concrete actions against the government he claimed to oppose that he shortly thereafter accepted a position working in it. It simply wouldn't do to disrupt the functioning of one's future employer, after all. The nature of Brown's own commitment can be readily contrasted to those he dismissed as "scruffy" in that many of *them* ultimately went underground and/or to prison in pursuit of their beliefs.

77. Ken Hurwitz, *Marching Nowhere* (New York: W. W. Norton, 1971).

78. Mairowitz, op. cit., pp. 221–26.

79. The best description of this development is found in Kirkpatrick Sale, *SDS* (New York: Vintage, 1974), pp. 455–600. A contending (and erroneous) thesis is offered in Alan Andelson, *SDS: A Profile* (New York: Charles Scribner's Sons, 1972), pp. 225-70. *See* also Thomas Powers, *Diana: The Making of a Terrorist* (New York: Houghton-Mifflin, 1971).

80. Michael Lerner, "Weatherman: The Politics of Despair," in *Weatherman,* Harold Jacobs, ed. (San Francisco: Ramparts Press, 1970), pp. 400–21.

81. Perhaps the preeminent topical articulation of this defection – an obvious precursor to the sort of swill later produced by Ellen Frankfort and Robin Morgan (*see* endnote 74) – accrues from another white feminist, Gail Sheehy, in her *Panthermania: The Clash of Black Against Black in One American City* (New York: Harper & Row, 1971).

82. For details, *see* Jo Durden-Smith, *Who Killed George Jackson: Fantasies, Paranoia and the Revolution* (New York: Alfred A. Knopf, 1976); Huey P. Newton, *War Against the Panthers: A Study of Repression in America* (Santa Cruz: Ph.D. Dissertation, Dept. of Philosophy, University of California, 1980); Ward Churchill and Jim Vander Wall, *The COINTELPRO Papers: Documents from the FBI's Secret Wars Against Dissent in the United States* (Boston: South End Press, 1990), esp. Chapt. 5.

83. There is nothing at all metaphorical intended by this statement. Leaving aside the obvious holocaust embodied in the institutionalization of slavery prior to the Civil War, *see,* e.g., Herbert Shapiro, *White Violence and Black Response: From Reconstruction to Montgomery* (Amherst: University of Massachusetts Press, 1988). For further details, *see* Stewart E. Tolnay and E. M. Beck, *A Festival of Violence: An Analysis of Southern Lynchings, 1882–1930* (Athens: University of Georgia Press, 1992); W. Fitzhugh Brundage, *Lynching in the New South: Georgia and Virginia, 1880–1930* (Urbana: University of Illinois Press, 1993).

84. Irv Kurki, speech to the Bradley University Peace Congress at Bradley University, Peoria, Illinois, 12 Dec. 1969 (tape on file). Kurki was at the time director of the local draft counseling office in Peoria and downstate Illinois organizer for the Resistance organization. His views in this regard were voiced in the wake of the December 4, 1969, assassination of Illinois Panther leaders Fred Hampton and Mark Clark (head of the Party's Peoria chapter) in Chicago. The sentiments are shared in Frankfort, op. cit., and elsewhere. For the best elaboration of what was known at the time about police operations to neutralize Hampton and the Party more generally – and, consequently, the extent to which statements such as Kurki's add up to conscious victim-blaming – see Roy Wilkins and Ramsey Clark et al., *Search and Destroy: A Report by the Commission of Inquiry into the Black Panthers and the Police* (New York: Metropolitan Applied Research Center, 1973). Further examination of the psychology involved will be found in William Ryan, *Blaming the Victim* (New York: Vintage, 1971).

85. There can be no question that the magnitude of slaughter in Indochina was known by American nonviolent oppositionists, even as it was occurring; *see*, e.g., David Dellinger, "Unmasking Genocide," *Liberation* (Dec. 1967/Jan. 1968). Given this understanding, which undeniably equates the posture of the U.S. government with that of the Third Reich, at least in some key respects, the pacifist response to the war in Indochina was tantamount to arguing that the appropriate response to nazism was *not* physical resistance. *See* again the above sections of this essay devoted to the implications of any such attitude for those targeted among extermination.

86. To take another example – this one concerning nineteenth-century white immigrant anarchists framed by police provocateurs in Chicago and subsequently executed by the State of Illinois – *see* Bradford Lyttle, *Haymarket: Violence Destroys a Movement* (New York: Committee for Nonviolent Action, 1965). For the reality of what occurred – rather than Lyttle's patently victim-blaming version of it – *see* Bernard R. Kogan, ed., *The Haymarket Riot* (Boston: D.C. Heath, 1959); and Henry David, *The Haymarket Affair* (New York: Collier, 1963).

87. Frantz Fanon covers this aspect of displacement in a section titled "French Intellectuals and Democrats and the Algerian Revolution," in *Toward the African Revolution* (New York: Grove Press, 1968), pp. 76-90.

88. In this sense, the term "responsible" should be considered as interchangeable with "respectable." Neither term is self-explanatory, al-

though they are invariably employed as if they were. The relevant questions which should always be posed when such characterizations come up are "responsible to *what*?" and "respected by *whom*?"

89. "Radical movements" which devote themselves to liberally-sanctioned causes like First Amendment rights, including those which appear temporarily most vibrant and energetic, are ultimately self-coopting and diversionary in terms of real social issues. Their "victories," in and of themselves, tend to reinforce rather than erode the functioning of the status quo; for a classic illustration, *see* David Lance Goines, *The Free Speech Movement: Coming of Age in the 1960s* (Berkeley: Ten Speed Press, 1993).

90. This is standard form in a liberal democracy, no matter how "conservative" its garb; *see* Thomas I. Emerson, *The System of Freedom of Expression* (New York: Random House, 1970); and Isaac Balbus, *The Dialectic of Legal Repression* (New York: Russel Sage Foundation, 1973).

91. An even more sophisticated approach was taken by West German counterterrorism expert Christian Ludtke in his advocacy of factoring a certain (containable) quantity of violence by the opposition into élite calculations of the costs of maintaining the status quo. His point was that the functioning of the modern state inherently generates such responses, and at least tacit support of them across a fairly wide spectrum of the public. By absorbing an "acceptable" level of activity by small clandestine groups like the Red Army Fraction without reacting in an overly repressive fashion, he argued, the state security apparatus could fashion a useful sociopolitical venting mechanism which serves to preempt more threatening forms or degrees of antistatist violence. Fortunately, the quality of Ludtke's reasoning – which, if adopted as policy might have had the effect of reducing the potential for armed struggle to little more than that of the "revolutionary theatre" already evident in the nonviolent movements of most liberal democracies – eluded the bulk of his rather duller counterparts; *see* generally, Peter J. Katzenstein, *West Germany's Internal Security Policy: State and Violence in the 1970s and 1980s* (Ithaca, New York: Center for Studies in International Affairs, Cornell University, 1990). With respect to the idea of militant political staging, in this case within what became the reformist wing of the Black Panther Party, *see* Robert Burstein, *Revolution As Theater: Notes on the New Radical Style* (New York: Liveright, 1971).

92. This notion of prefiguration is featured as a prominent aspect of much past and current pacifist theory; *see,* e.g., Sharp, *Social Power and Political Freedom,* op. cit.; and Epstein, op. cit.

93. This does not have to be so. As Gramsci and a number of

subsequent theorists have demonstrated, prefigurative revelations serve a crucial function within the context of revolutionary struggle. But saying this is to say something rather different than that they can supplant such struggle; *see*, e.g., Abbie Hoffman, *Woodstock Nation* (New York: Vintage, 1969); and Jerry Rubin, *We Are Everywhere* (New York: Harper & Row, 1971). For a good summary of Gramsci's thinking on the matter, *see* Carl Boggs, *The Two Revolutions: Gramsci and the Dilemmas of Western Marxism* (Boston: South End Press, 1984), especially pp. 289-91. *See* also Walter L. Adamson, *Hegemony and Revolution: A Study of Antonio Gramsci's Political and Cultural Theory* (Berkeley: University of California Press, 1980), especially pp. 207–22.

94. The psychosocial and political bases for this were well articulated by the early 1970s; *see*, e.g., Eldridge Cleaver, *Soul on Ice* (San Francisco/New York: Ramparts/McGraw-Hill, 1968), and *Post-Prison Writings and Speeches* (San Francisco/New York: Ramparts/Random House, 1969); George L. Jackson, *Soledad Brother: The Prison Letters of George Jackson* (New York: Coward-McCann, 1970), and *Blood in My Eye* (New York: Random House, 1972). The conditions generating such sentiments have not changed much since then; *see* Alfonso Pinkney, *The Myth of Black Progress* (Cambridge: Cambridge University Press, 1984); Manning Marable, *The Crisis of Color and Democracy* (Monroe, Maine: Common Courage, 1992).

95. The relationship is not unlike that described by Angela Davis, bell hooks, and others as existing between women of colour and white feminism; Angela Y. Davis, *Women, Race & Class* (New York: Random House, 1981); bell hooks, *Ain't I A Woman: Black Women and Feminism* (Boston: South End Press, 1981), and *Yearning: Race, Gender and Cultural Politics* (Boston: South End Press, 1990); and Elena Featherston, ed., *Skin Deep: Women Writing on Color, Culture and Identity* (Freedom, California: Crossing Press, 1994).

96. Words are being put in no one's mouth here. Anyone doubting American pacifism's pretensions to status as a revolutionary (rather than reformist) doctrine should *see* David Dellinger, *Revolutionary Nonviolence* (New York: Bobbs-Merrill, 1971). If a strawman is set up by use of such terms, pacifists themselves constructed it.

97. *See* Jacques Ellul, *Propaganda: The Formation of Men's Attitudes* (New York: Alfred A. Knopf, 1965).

98. Dellinger, *Vietnam Revisited*, op. cit.

99. *See* Paul Joseph, *Cracks in the Empire: State Politics in the Vietnam War* (Boston: South End Press, 1981), pp. 245–86.

100. MacClear, op. cit., p. 200.

101. One of the more interesting takes on this is offered by Norman Mailer in *Miami and the Siege of Chicago: An Informal History of the Republican and Democratic Conventions of 1968* (New York: Primus, 1986; reprint of 1968 original).

102. MacLear, op. cit., pp. 229–30.

103. Richard Boyle, *Flower of the Dragon: The Breakdown of the U.S. Army in Vietnam* (San Francisco: Ramparts Press, 1972); Cincinnatus, *Self-Destruction: The Breakdown and Decay of the United States Army During the Vietnam Era* (New York: W. W. Norton, 1981); Col. David E. Hackworth, *About Face: The Odyssey of an American Warrior* (New York: Simon & Schuster, 1989).

104. It is an interesting commentary on the depth of American liberal racism that after the killings of literally hundreds of Afroamerican activists by police and military personnel – including quite a number of black college students – responsible establishment types were finally upset when four white kids were gunned down by the National Guard on a Middle-American campus; James A. Michener, *Kent State: What Happened and Why* (New York: Random House/Reader's Digest, 1971).

105. In some ways, the weight of this policy shift fell even harder on Cambodia; William Shawcross, *Sideshow: Kissinger, Nixon and the Destruction of Cambodia* (New York: Simon & Schuster, 1979).

106. Tiziano Terzani, *Giai Phong! The Fall and Liberation of Saigon* (New York: St. Martin's Press, 1976); Van Tien Dung, *Our Great Spring Victory* (London: Monthly Review Press, 1977); and Wilfred Burchett, *Grasshoppers and Elephants: Why Vietnam Fell* (New York: Urizen, 1977).

107. As the marxist intellectual Isaac Deutscher put it to David Dellinger and A. J. Muste in a 1969 discussion of strategy and tactics, "One might say there is an inconsistency in your attitude, a contradiction in your preaching nonviolence and yet accepting morally . . . the violence applied by the Vietcong in Vietnam and probably by the FLN in Algeria"; "Marxism and Nonviolence," *Liberation* (July 1969).

108. Dellinger, *Revolutionary Nonviolence*, op. cit.; Sharp, *The Dynamics of Nonviolent Action*, op. cit.; Staughton Lynd, ed., *Nonviolence in America: A Documentary History* (Indianapolis: Bobbs-Merrill, 1966). For another broad articulation, *see* Richard Gregg, *The Power of Nonviolence* (New York: Schocken, 1966).

109. Dating accrues from the point of initial publication of Lenin's *Imperialism: The Highest Stage of Capitalism* in Zürich; widely read at

the time, the pamphlet has seen continuous reprinting/distribution ever since.

110. There is by now a vast literature on the subject, either positing the thesis directly or strongly implying it. The work of Harry Magdoff, André Gunder Frank, Immanuel Wallerstein, Richard Barnett, Eduardo Galeano, and Regis Debray (to list only six prominent examples) each falls within this classification, albeit on the basis of a wide range of precepts and motivations.

111. E.g., the 1961 Declaration on the Granting of Independence to Colonial Countries and Peoples (U.N.G.A. 1514 (XV), 14 Dec. 1960); Burns H. Weston, Richard A. Falk, and Anthony D'Amato, eds., *Basic Documents in International Law and World Order* (St. Paul, Minnesota: West, 1990), pp. 343–44.

112. A seminal advancement of this view within the United States (new) left of the '60s is found in Carl Oglesby, "An Essay on the Meanings of the Cold War," in *Containment and Change: Two Dissenting Views of American Foreign Policy*, Carl Oglesby and Richard Schaull, eds. (New York: Macmillan, 1967), pp. 157–69. The idea was taken in a rather unintended direction by Karen Ashley et al., "You Don't Need a Weatherman to Know Which Way the Wind Blows," *New Left Notes* (18 June 1969), reprinted in Jacobs, op. cit., pp. 51–90.

113. Two (among very many) elaborations of this view from the Third World itself may be found in Frantz Fanon, *A Dying Colonialism* (New York: Grove Press, 1965); and Vo Nguyen Giap, *People's War, People's Army* (New York: Praeger, 1962).

114. *See* Jean Paul Sartre, "Preface," in Frantz Fanon, *The Wretched of the Earth* (New York: Grove Press, 1966), pp. 7–26.

115. *See* Michael Carver, *War Since 1945* (New York: Putnam and Sons, 1981).

116. For a lucid articulation of this principle, *see* Joseph, op. cit., especially pp. 43–74. On military doctrines, *see* Major John S. Pustay, *Counterinsurgency Warfare* (New York: Free Press, 1965); Michael T. Klare and Peter Kornbluh, eds., *Low Intensity Warfare: Counterinsurgency, Proinsurgency, and Antiterrorism in the Eighties* (New York: Pantheon, 1988).

117. Such a proposition, loosely termed "strangulation theory," was quite broadly discussed within the new left during the period 1967–1969 and found perhaps its clearest expression in Bill Ayers, "A Strategy to Win," *New Left Notes* (12 Sept. 1969), reprinted in Jacobs, op. cit., pp. 183–95. It is quite instructive to note that much of the criticism of the

undertakings of Weatherman and similar groups by the left was that their actions were "premature" (*see* Lerner, op. cit.). There also seems to have been a particular horror that it was *white* radicals who were resorting to armed struggle. The whole debate appears to rest, at bottom, on a perverse extension of Maoist principles of revolutionary warfare from the national to the geopolitical realm; *see* Mao's *On Protracted War* (Peking: Foreign Languages Press, 1977).

118. For development of the concept of internal colonialism in a manner which can be readily extrapolated to North America, *see* Michael Hector, *Internal Colonialism: The Celtic Fringe in British National Development, 1536–1966* (Berkeley: University of California Press, 1975). With regard to positioning for armed struggle, *see* Abraham Guillén, *Philosophy of the Urban Guerrilla* (New York: William Morrow, 1973); and Carlos Marighella, *Mini-Manual of the Urban Guerrilla* (Boulder, Colorado: Paladin Press, 1985, reprint of 1967 original).

119. This is a pronounced trend in American leftist thinking. For just one among many possible examples, *see* Steve Rosskamm Shalom, ed., *Socialist Visions* (Boston: South End Press, 1983).

120. Exactly why is it that the Third World is supposed to bear the brunt of destroying colonialist power while the "opposition" within the colonizing powers essentially sits by waiting for "the moment"? How this bloody task is to be completed is never quite explained. The question of why it would not be more appropriate for mother country radicals to bloody themselves going after the *source* of the problem while the Third World's busy themselves prefiguring the outcome is apparently not considered a polite conversational topic by the American left. *See,* e.g., Adam Roberts, *Civilian Resistance as a National Defense: Non-Violent Action Against Aggression* (Harrisburg, Pennsylvania: Stackpole Books, 1968), p. 57.

121. The kind of appropriation involved occurs intellectually as well as materially. For a classic example of the former, *see* Jerry Mander's *In the Absence of the Sacred: The Failure of Technology and the Survival of the Indian Nations* (San Francisco: Sierra Club Books, 1991).

122. Witness, as but one example, that Gene Sharp's "revolutionary" tract, *Social Power and Political Freedom* (op. cit.) is introduced by no less than Senator Mark O. Hatfield.

123. For a very sharp framing of the question of white-skin privilege, *see* Lee Lockwood, *A Conversation with Eldridge Cleaver in Algiers* (New York: Delta, 1970).

124. As Lucy Dawidowicz puts it, "Civil disobedience as a strategy

of political opposition can succeed only with a government ruled by conscience"; *War Against the Jews*, op. cit., p. 371. The assumption of American pacifism – contra evidence such as its endorsement of black chattel slavery, expropriation of the northern half of Mexico, Hawai'i, Puerto Rico, and the Philippines, and genocide of American Indians and Filipinos during the nineteenth century – has always been that the U.S. government is such an entity. In addition to the works already cited, *see* also Clarence Marsh Case, *Nonviolent Coercion: A Study in the Methods of Social Pressure* (New York: Century, 1923); Theodor Paullin, *Introduction to Nonviolence* (Philadelphia: Pacifist Research Bureau, 1944); Gene Sharp, *Exploring Nonviolent Alternatives* (Boston: Porter Sargent, 1960); Harvey Seiffert, *Conquest by Suffering: The Prospects and Process of Nonviolent Resistance* (Philadelphia: Westminster, 1965); A. Paul Hare and Herbert H. Blumburg, eds., *Nonviolent Direct Action: American Cases: Social-Psychological Analyses* (Cleveland: Corpus Books, 1968).

125. The process has hardly been restricted to Germany. For a summary of its application in Spain, *see* Hugh Thomas, *The Spanish Civil War* (New York: Harper & Row, 1961), esp. pp. 1–116; for Italy, *see* Richard Collier, *Duce! A Biography of Benito Mussolini* (New York: Viking, 1971), esp. pp. 83–133; for the USSR, *see* Robert Conquest, *The Great Terror: Stalin's Purge of the Thirties* (New York: Macmillan, 1968). That the United States has already flirted with the same process, even at the very height of its power, is amply evidenced in Victory S. Navasky, *Naming Names* (New York: Penguin, 1981); *see* also David Caute's *The Great Fear: The Anti-Communist Purge Under Truman and Eisenhower* (New York: Simon & Schuster, 1978).

126. It should be recalled that the Jews were not the only, or even the first, "enemies of the state" targeted by the nazis. Dachau and similar concentration camps were originally opened in the mid-1930s to house communists, socialists, social democrats, key trade unionists, *pacifists,* and homosexuals. *See* Helmut Krausnik et al., op. cit., pp. 145–214; and Hohne, op. cit., pp. 199–204.

127. Bettelheim, op. cit., p. x; on the "it can't happen here" syndrome, *see* Bud Schultz and Ruth Schultz, *It Did Happen Here: Recollections of Political Repression in America* (Berkeley: University of California Press, 1989).

128. Bettelheim, op. cit., p. xi.

129. *See*, e.g., Erik H. Erikson and Huey P. Newton, *In Search of Common Ground* (New York: W. W. Norton, 1973).

130. This outcome runs exactly counter to the rationalist expectations so optimistically posited by Jürgen Habermas in his *Knowledge and Human Interests* (Boston: Beacon Press, 1971). It comes much closer to the sort of irrationality disguised as rational opinion described by Russell Jacoby in *Social Amnesia: A Critique of Conformist Psychology from Adler to Lang* (Boston: Beacon Press, 1976).

131. This leaves aside the Eastern traditions of Hindu and Buddhist pacifism, which in certain variants fuse theology and politics in the manner described; *see,* e.g., Adam Roberts, "Buddhism and Politics in South Vietnam," *The World Today,* Vol. 21, No. 6 (June 1965). In the West, we also find subsets which fit this pattern; *see,* e.g., Margaret E. Hirst, *The Quakers in Peace and War* (New York: George H. Doran, 1923). Usually, however, we find a much shallower, less consistent and more opportunistic expression of such thinking in the U.S.; *see,* e.g., William Robert Miller, *Nonviolence: A Christian Interpretation* (New York: Association Press, 1964).

132. *See,* for example, Wilhelm Reich, *The Mass Psychology of Fascism* (New York: Farrar, Straus and Giroux, 1971). On the other side of the ideological coin, *see* Richard Crossman, *The God That Failed* (New York: Harper, 1950).

133. *See* Eric Hoffer, *The True Believer* (New York: Harper & Row, 1951). *See* also Reich, op. cit. At another level, *see* Max Weber, *The Protestant Ethic and the Spirit of Capitalism* (New York: Charles Scribner's Sons, 1958).

134. *See* Gould, "Taxonomy As Politics: The Harm of False Classification," *Dissent* (Winter 1990).

135. The point can be illustrated anecdotally almost infinitely. For just one example, there is a matter which occurred at the 1982 Midwest Radical Therapy Conference near Boone, Iowa. Here, a noted "pacifist feminist," who quite consistently and vocally prided herself on never having lifted a finger in physical opposition to such state policies as oppression of the domestic black community or genocide in Southeast Asia, and who was quite arrogant in her superior disassociation from those who did not share her "correct" vision of political appropriateness in this regard, proceeded to physically assault a black man who failed to extinguish his cigarette when she instructed him to do so. Similar examples are legion.

136. *See* Joel Kovel, *White Racism: A Psychohistory* (New York: Pantheon, 1970).

137. John Tomlinson, *Cultural Imperialism* (Baltimore: Johns Hopkins University Press, 1991); The process works as well in reverse as it

does when projected into the future; Robert Young, *White Mythologies: Writing History and the West* (London/New York: Routledge, 1990).

138. Donald L. Nathanson, *Shame and Pride* (New York: W. W. Norton, 1992).

139. With only a minor reinterpretation, this point becomes an essential subtext of both Reich and Marcuse; Paul A. Robinson, *The Freudian Left: Wilhelm Reich, Geza Roheim, Herbert Marcuse* (New York: Harper & Row, 1969).

140. Hilberg, op. cit., 1961 edition, pp. 219–23.

141. For example, *The Compact Edition of the Oxford English Dictionary* (1971 ed.) defines praxis as "doing, acting, action, practice."

142. *See* Lawrence S. Stepelevich, "August von Cieszkowski: From Theory to Praxis," *History and Theory*, Vol. XIII, No. 1 (Winter 1974), pp. 39-52. The quotation actually derives from Cieszkowski's *Prolegomena zur Historiosophie*, published in Berlin, 1838.

143. Karl Marx, "Theses on Feuerbach," in *Karl Marx: Selected Writings in Sociology and Social Philosophy*, T. Bottomore and M. Rubel, eds. (New York: Penguin, 1967), p. 83.

144. Karl Marx, *The Poverty of Philosophy* (New York: International, 1969), p. 173.

145. G. W. F. Hegel, *The Philosophy of History*, J. Sibree, trans. (New York: Dover, 1956), p. 33.

146. Richard Kilminster, *Praxis and Method: A Sociological Dialogue with Lukacs, Gramsci and the Early Frankfurt School* (London: Routledge & Keegan Paul, 1979), pp. 264–65.

147. This sentiment goes, of course, to Marx's famous pronouncement that the object of theory "is not to understand history, but to change it," later recast by Lenin as the dictum that "without revolutionary theory there can be no revolutionary practice."

148. This is as opposed to the continuing elaboration of and increasingly esoteric preoccupation with "grand theory": critical theory in the manner of Herbert Marcuse and Jürgen Habermas (as well as the "Adorno revival"), semiotic theory in the manner of Umberto Eco and Jean Baudrillard, structuralist theory in the manner of Louis Althusser, and so on. It is also as opposed to journalistic sorts of endeavors recounting the concrete aspects of various liberatory struggles without attempting to extrapolate formal tenets of tactical praxis for application elsewhere.

149. As Deutscher (op. cit.) observed, "It is said that Marxism suits the underdeveloped countries but not the advanced and industrial

west." In effect, Marx is stood squarely on his head insofar as he was clear that his notion of revolution could *only* occur in the *most* advanced countries.

150. Léon Trotsky, *The History of the Russian Revolution* (New York: Pathfinder, 1971 edition); Jerome Ch'en, *Mao and the Chinese Revolution* (London: Oxford University Press, 1967); Che Guevara, *Guerrilla Warfare* (New York: Monthly Review, 1961); Joseph Kraft, *The Struggle for Algeria* (New York: Doubleday, 1961); Henri Weber, *Nicaragua: The Sandinista Revolution* (London: Verso, 1981); and David Martin and Phyllis Johnson, *The Struggle for Zimbabwe* (New York: Monthly Review Press, 1981).

151. Ernest Harsh and Tony Thomas, *Angola: The Hidden History of Washington's War* (New York: Pathfinder, 1976); Gérard Chaliand, *Armed Struggle in Africa: With the Guerrillas in "Portuguese" Guinea* (New York: Monthly Review Press, 1969); Richard Leonard, *South Africa at War: White Power and Crisis in Southern Africa* (Westport, Connecticut: Lawrence Hill, 1983); John Ya-Otto, *Battlefront Namibia* (Westport, Connecticut: Lawrence Hill, 1981); Maria Esther Gilio, *The Tupamaros Guerrillas: The Structure and Strategy of the Urban Guerrilla Movement* (New York: Saturday Review, 1970); Neill Macaulay, *The Prestes Column: Revolution in Brazil* (New York: New Viewpoints, 1974); Simon Strong, *Shining Path: Terror and Revolution in Peru* (New York: Random House, 1992). For the most topical survey of the Western Hemisphere, *see* Liza Gross, *Handbook of Leftist Guerrilla Groups in Latin America and the Caribbean* (Boulder, Colorado: Westview Press, 1995).

152. Concerning Fanon's theoretics in this regard, *see* Marie B. Perinbam, *Holy Violence: The Revolutionary Thought of Frantz Fanon* (Washington, D.C.: Three Continents Press, 1982); *see* also Irene L. Gendzier, *Frantz Fanon: A Critical Study* (New York: Vantage Books, 1974), especially "The Question of Violence," pp. 195–205. On Guevara, *see* his *Guerrilla Warfare* (op. cit.); *see* also Michael Lowy, *The Marxism of Che Guevara* (New York: Monthly Review Press, 1973), especially "Part III: Guerrilla Warfare," pp. 75–112. For Mao, *see* his *On Protracted War* (Peking: Foreign Languages Press, 1967); *see* also Stanley Karnow, *Mao and China: From Revolution to Revolution* (New York: Viking, 1972), especially Chapt. 12, "Out of the Barrel of a Gun," pp. 276–96. Concerning Giap, *see* his *People's War, People's Army* (New York: Praeger, 1962).

153. Blase Bonpane, *Guerrillas for Peace: Liberation Theology and the Central American Revolution* (Boston: South End Press, 1985), p. 1.

154. *Ibid.*, p. 8.

155. Significant portions of the Italian left have renounced non-violence as a strategy or method altogether. *See* Allesandro Silj, *Never Again Without a Rifle: The Origins of Italian Terrorism*, Salvator Attanasio, trans. (New York: Karz, 1979).

156. It is instructive that practitioners of armed struggle from the Third World context are also quite vociferously condemned when they are audacious enough to carry violence into the very industrialized nations objectively responsible for their colonization. The clearest examples here are the extreme equivocation with which the Palestinian Liberation Organization is treated by most of the left within late capitalist societies and the outright revulsion visited by progressives upon Muammar Qathaffi concerning his practice of exporting violence back to the societies with the clearest record(s) of engendering it. The same principle applies, of course, to colonized First World nationalities such as the Irish, Basques, and Quebequois when their military/political organizations – e.g., the IRA – practice the same sort of "turn around" tactics. This all corroborates the notion that the "mother country opposition" considers it a "right" to be exempted from direct violence in any form. On the movements mentioned, *see* Assata Shakur, *Assata: An Autobiography* (Westport, Connecticut: Lawrence Hill, 1987); Ronald Fernandez, *Los Macheteros* (New York: Prentice Hall, 1987); Peter Matthiessen, *In the Spirit of Crazy Horse* (New York: Viking, 2nd. ed., 1991); Tim Pat Coogan, *The IRA: A History* (New York: Roberts Rinehart, 1993); Robert P. Clark, *Negotiating with ETA: Obstacles to Peace in Basque Country, 1975–1988* (Reno: University of Nevada Press, 1990); and Tom Vague, *Televisionaries: The Red Army Faction Story, 1963–1993* (San Francisco: AK Press, 1994).

157. Tony Geraghty, *Inside the SAS* (London: Arms and Armor Press, 1980).

158. Robert Taber, *War of the Flea: How Guerrilla Fighters Could Win the World* (New York: Cidatel Press, 1970); and Robert B. Asprey, *War in the Shadows: The Guerrilla in History* (New York: Doubleday, 1975), esp. Vol. II.

159. For an interesting examination of "terrorist" thinking and methods, as well as adequate reconstruction of its application between 1970 and 1995 – albeit within a rather reactionary ideological framework – *see* Roberta Goren, *The Soviet Union and Terrorism* (London/Boston: George Allen & Unwin, 1984). Ideological balance can be obtained through Edward S. Herman's *The Real Terror Network* (Boston: South End Press, 1984).

160. The ineffectuality of the United States and other neocolonialist

powers in attempting to offset the proliferation of guerrilla wars since 1950, creating "counterinsurgency" doctrine and units, is evident in a number of studies. A sampling would include Col. Charlie A. Beckwith, *Delta Force* (London: Fontana/Collins, 1983); Lt. Col. Anthony B. Herbert, with James T. Wooten, *Soldier* (New York: Holt, Reinhart & Winston, 1973); and Donald Duncan, *The New Legions* (New York: Random House, 1967).

161. Louis Althusser, *For Marx* (New York: Vintage Books, 1970), p. 251: "Generalities I are abstract, part-ideological, part-scientific generalities that are the raw material of science . . . "

162. Ernest Gellner, "Foreword," in J. G. Merquoir, *The Veil and the Mask: Essays on Culture and Ideology* (London: Routledge & Kegan Paul, 1979), p. 2.

163. Merquoir, op. cit., p. 29.

164. Those confused about the distinction inhering between reform and revolution might wish to consult John and Barbara Ehrenreich's "From Resistance to Revolution," *Monthly Review* (April 1968). Another useful perspective can be found in the section entitled "Rebellion and Revolution," in George Katsiaficas' *The Imagination of the New Left: A Global Analysis of 1968* (Boston: South End Press, 1987), pp. 179–86.

165. Kwame Turé (Stokely Carmichael), speech at the Auraria Campus Student Center, Denver, Colorado, 24 Nov. 1985 (tape on file).

166. Put another way, it is simply to gain a different sort of appreciation of Karl von Clausewitz's famous dictum that war is merely politics pursued by other means. Conversely, politics would be war pursued in the same manner.

167. The same principle, of course, is inversely applicable to those who would insist that armed struggle/terror is the "*only* appropriate means" of confronting state power under advanced capitalism. However, the scant number of those professing such a belief in the United States – especially as opposed to the numbers of people advocating nonviolence as an absolute – tends to speak for itself in terms of the emphasis accorded each problem in this essay.

168. *See* Nicos Poulantzas, *Fascism and Dictatorship: The Third International and the Problem of Fascism* (London: Verso, 1979), especially "Forms of the Ideological Crisis: The Crisis of Revolutionary Organizations," pp. 143–46. Outcomes are posited, however unintendedly, in Bertram Gross, *Friendly Fascism: The Face of Power in America* (Boston: South End Press, 1982).

169. The term is employed within its precise rather than its popu-

larized meaning, i.e., from the Greek *radic*, meaning "source" or "root." The radical therapist is one who pursues problems to their root or source. The psychological analysis and approach taken is that sketched out in Jerome Angel, ed., *The Radical Therapist* (New York: Ballantine, 1971), and *Rough Times* (New York: Ballantine, 1973).

170. This requirement may well lead to the application of a variation of the principle posited by Frank Black Elk in his "Observations on Marxism and the Lakota Tradition," in *Marxism and Native Americans*, Ward Churchill, ed. (Boston: South End Press, 1983), pp. 137–56; people who are not typically considered as therapists – and who may well not even perceive themselves as such – will be needed to provide therapy to many self-proclaimed radical therapists before the latter can hope to extend assistance to others.

171. A quick sample of some of the best: Kurt Saxon, *The Poor Man's James Bond* (Eureka, California: Atlan Formularies, 1975); Lt. Col. Anthony B. Herbert, *The Soldier's Handbook* (Englewood, California: Cloverleaf Books, 1979); William Ewart Fairburn, *Scientific Self-Defense* (San Francisco: Interservice, 1982); and Tony Lesce and Jo-Anne Lesce, *Checklist for Survival* (Cornville, Arizona: Desert Publications, 1983). Copy machines are, of course, a handy aid in furthering dissemination – and to avert putting undue revenue into the hands of the right. This is not to mention the incredible range of official military training and field manuals (e.g., *Ranger Training Manual; Special Forces Handbook; Booby Traps, Escape and Evasion; Explosives and Demolitions;* and *Your M-16 Rifle*) available by law at essentially no charge through the U.S. Government Printing Office in Washington, D.C.

172. This is to reiterate Che Guevara's contention, "at the risk of sounding ridiculous," that the true revolutionary is guided by a sense of love rather than hate, and that "to love, one must fight"; Michael Lowy, *The Marxism of Che Guevara* (op.cit. p. 54). Or, to return to Isaac Deutscher (op. cit.): "There is a whole dialectic of violence and nonviolence implied in the Marxist doctrine from its beginnings . . . As Marxists, we have always preached . . . the need to overthrow capitalism by force [yet retain] the aspiration to transform societies in such a way that violence should cease forever as the necessary and permanent element in the regulation of the relationship between society and individuals, between individuals and individuals. In embracing the vision of a nonviolent society, Marxism . . . has gone further and deeper than any pacifist preachers of nonviolence have ever done. Why? Because Marxism has laid bare the roots of violence

in our society, which the others have not done. Marxism has set out to attack those roots; to uproot violence not just from human thoughts, not just from human emotions, but to uproot [it] from the very bases of the material existence of society." Although myself strongly anti-marxist in my political perspectives and practice, I must admit that on these points I wholeheartedly concur with the views expressed.

On Ward Churchill's "Pacifism as Pathology": Toward a Consistent Revolutionary Practice

by Mike Ryan

It is important to explain how I come to be debating Ward Churchill's essay "Pacifism as Pathology." While I endorse as accurate the basic tenets of Churchill's argument, I am not speaking for Ward Churchill; I am only attempting to use Churchill's paper as a starting point for an analysis of where we find ourselves in Canada today.

In Montréal, where I live, I've been involved since 1978 in what is now called civil disobedience, having chalked up five arrests engaging in rather peculiar behavior. These years of sporadic involvement with non-violent resistance have left me totally disillusioned with the activity of the peace movement in Canada on virtually every possible level.

Some Definitions

To begin to seriously discuss our common points and our differences, I think it is necessary that we have shared definitions. Much of the debate these days, pro and con pacifism and nonviolence, is, it appears to me, skewed by a near total lack of common language. I therefore offer specific definitions of key terms as I use them.

Regarding pacifism, I accept Churchill's definition of true pacifism: a belief that precludes infliction of violence upon others, but which does not bar the absorption of violence by adherents.[1]

Regarding nonviolence, I use a definition offered by Kelly Booth: "Mutual bending and fitting is the very essence of nonviolence."[2]

And, regarding violence, I again draw upon Booth: "Violence is the imposing of a form, or a set of conditions, on another party without regards to the others' interests, or without sensitivity to their situation."[3]

Arguments for Nonviolence

Arguments for nonviolence seem to fall into two basic categories: ideological and practical. The ideological arguments stress an alleged moral superiority of nonviolence. Essentially, this argument holds that nonviolence is good (right) and violence is bad (wrong). Hence, if we want to be good (in the right), we are morally bound to behave in a nonviolent way.

Along with this basic ideological concept, there is

a series of practical arguments against violence used to buttress the moral argument or, in the case of nonviolent activists who are not bound to pacifism, used as arguments against violence in their own right. There are four basic arguments in this category:

1. There is the ever-popular assertion that the time is not right.

2. It is contended that violence alienates the people.

3. It is suggested that violence brings down repression (a kind of practical reworking of the old moral argument that violence begets violence).

4. Lastly, we are told violence will get us bad press.

To respond to the argument that the time is not right, allow me to turn to an article by Dr. Rosalie Bertell printed in the Cruise Missile Conversion Project's 1984 pamphlet, *A Case for NonViolent Resistance.* In *Early War Crimes of World War III*, Dr. Bertell estimates that if one begins counting with the Hiroshima and Nagasaki bombings, there have already been more than twenty million victims of what she calls the early stages of World War III. She adds:

> The prognosis for the world, given this self-destructive and earth-destructive behavior, is poor. As nuclear powers increase their own pollution because of distorted military short term thinking, the people of their nations will give birth to more physically damaged offspring. These offspring will be

less able to cope with the increasingly hazardous environment. Thus, a death process is under way, even if there is no catastrophic accident or nuclear holocaust. Just like individual reactions to personal death, so society reacts to species death with the typical stages of denial, anger, barter and finally, it is hoped, realism. For those who have reached the fourth stage there is no pretense that things are normal or one must believe the experts. The stance is to attempt to heal the possibility of mortal wounds, or sit with the dying earth. Honesty is the fundamental medicinal approach.[4]

Given this reality, I am prompted to ask how bad conditions must become before we recognize that the time is right for any and all forms of resistance that can be effectual in putting an end to this madness, before it puts an end to us.

Turning now to the argument that violence alienates the people, I find myself face to face with several unanswerable flaws of logic. If violence alienates the people, are we to refrain from engaging in any but passive acts of protest (and here I use the term protest rather than resistance quite consciously) because this will win popular support? If this is the case, I am forced to ask why, after years of consistent nonviolent protest, no qualitative growth, and only the slightest quantitative, has occurred within our movement? From these questions, I would go on to suggest that catering our activity to our perception (which might not even be accurate) of the level of resistance acceptable to people, far from being revolutionary, is in fact counter to the development of revolutionary consciousness:

> A party (or, in our case, an organization or movement) which *bases itself* on an *existing* average level of consciousness and activity, will end up *reducing* the present level of both. It is the party's responsibility to *lead*, to *change* the existing level of consciousness and activity, raise them to higher levels.[5]

It is clear that the peace movement, rather than offering vital connections and a direction for popular discontent (which plainly exists), has failed to offer anything more than a repetitive and increasingly boring spectacle. The government in Ottawa, and the general populus, has increasingly taken to yawning at our activities.

The argument that violence brings repression down on the left indicates a *naïveté* bordering on sheer madness. Do we *really* believe that if we could devise a non-violent means of eliminating the state we would be allowed to proceed unhindered in carrying it out? The state is violent in its very nature. The police, the army, and prisons stand as immediate, tangible evidence of this. The genocide of Third and Fourth World peoples stands as evidence of this. Canada's role as an arms producer and supplier for the Indonesian colonization of East Timor is a daily, ongoing act of violence. Violence, overt and covert, aggressive and preventive, is fundamental to the function of the Canadian state. No violence issuing from the movement could hope to be more than a pale reflection of the constant violence of the repressive apparati. That this violence generally remains invisible is more a statement of our failure than of our success, a reflection of the degree to which we have remained within the limits acceptable to the state. As Mao said in 1939:

> It is good and not bad if the enemy fights against us: I think it is bad for us – be it for individual, a party, an army, or a school of thought – if the enemy does not take a stand against us, because in that case it could only mean that we are hand in glove with the enemy. If we are being fought by the enemy, then that is good: it is proof that we have drawn a clear line between us and the enemy. If the enemy goes vigorously into action against us, and accepts nothing at all, then this is even better: it shows that we have not only drawn a clear line between us and the enemy, but that our work has achieved tremendous success.

Finally, and intimately connected to the idea that violence creates state repression, is the equally curious concept that violence gets the movement bad press (presumably reinforcing the alienation of the people). One wonders how it could be believed that any kind of consistent good press can be expected from media owned by the same corporate interests we are attacking.

To turn from the ideological, or moral, argument favoring nonviolence, an argument I personally believe to be more worthy of respect than the tactical argument(s) is the examination of our relationship to the international struggle and to other peoples struggling for freedom within the borders of North America. When nonviolence is proposed as the only acceptable form of resistance by white militants in North American, it is not, for me, a statement of moral depth, but a statement regarding the depth of their white skin privilege.

Our situation as white radicals, and this is especially true for white men, is that of people who, for one reason or another, have chosen to partially break from the oppressor nation we are part of. The conscious choice to break with our culture does not *de facto* remove the privilege of our position. The very existence of a choice between resistance and acceptance – the fact that all white resisters can ultimately return to the fold – colours our perceptions of both ourselves and of resistance from the outset. The simple choice to resist does not change our perception, if, in fact, it can ever be changed, or remove our white skin privilege.

In the pamphlet *Pornography, Rape, War: Making the Links*, coproduced in 1984 by the Women's Action for Peace and the Alliance for NonViolent Action, this privilege is explicitly recognized, but in a way that reinforces it:

> As part of a white, middle-class society, we are privileged with some degree of basic humyn rights, respect for humyn dignity, and the possibility of making effective changes through nonviolent means.[6]

This, apparently, leads to three responsibilities:

First it is our responsibility not to escalate the extent of the use of violence; secondly, it is our responsibility to respond in such a way that recognizes the original fact – that no peoples would choose a violent struggle unless they deemed it necessary for their survival – and our specific privileged capacity to effect change through nonviolent means; thirdly, it is both our capacity and our responsibility to develop and extend the credibility of a commitment to nonviolent responses and resolutions to oppressive conditions.[7]

What is here referred to varyingly as the possibility of making effective changes through nonviolent means and our specific privileged capacity to effect change through nonviolent means is, in fact, more accurately a recognition of our capacity to live without change because our privileged position not only makes that possible, but relatively comfortable.

Here I think that the politics of the comfort zone, as Churchill describes them, hold true for what we are experiencing in the Canadian peace movement. Allow me to quote a section:

The question central to the emergence and maintenance of nonviolence as the oppositional fundament of American activism has been, by and large, not the truly pacifist formulation, "How can we forge a revolutionary politics within which we can avoid inflicting violence on others?" On the contrary, a more accurate articulation would be, "What sort of politics might I engage in which will both allow me to posture as a progressive *and* allow me to avoid incurring harm to *myself*?" Hence, the trappings of pacifism have been subverted to establish a sort of politics of the comfort zone, not only akin to what Bettelheim termed the philosophy of business as usual and devoid of perceived risk to its advocates, but minus any conceivable revolutionary impetus as well. The intended revolutionary content of true pacifist activism of the sort practiced by the Gandhian movement, the Berrigans and Norman Morrison, is thus isolated and subsumed in the U.S., even among the ranks of self-professing participants.[8]

It seems, in short, that the civil disobedience of the white Canadian peace movement, rather than being a revolutionary practice or an honest expression of protest, has become a form of catharsis, a practice that allows us to cleanse our souls of the guilt of our white skin privilege for ourselves and for each other without posing a threat either to the state or ourselves. We create a theatre of pseudoresistance in which everyone has their part. We dutifully announce the time, place, and form of our resistance. The police will report for duty at the appointed time and place. We will sit down and refuse to move until X change occurs in government policy. A pseudodiscourse will occur between the police and the protesters. The media will take some photos and possibly prepare a short report. The police will make inevitable arrests. If all goes smoothly (and, if we have our way, it will), the whole spectacle will be over in under an hour, sometimes as quickly as fifteen minutes.

If just the farce of this theatre piece were under consideration, I would be content to call it a living tragicomedy, have myself an ironic laugh, and forget it. Unfortunately, one must also consider the underlying message, for it is at this level that our interests and those of the state, sadly enough, coincide. We are attempting to demonstrate the existence of opposition to state policy. Far from wanting to silence this opposition, however, the state can thrive on it if the message is the right one. The message of civil disobedience as it is now practiced is this: There is opposition in society. The state deals with this opposition firmly but gently, *according to the law*. Unlike some countries, *Canada is a democratic society which tolerates opposition*. Therefore, it is unnecessary for anyone to step outside the forms of protest accepted by this society; *it is unnecessary to resist*.

Do we really believe the state allows small groups to engage in openly planned and publicized protest actions because it is somehow powerless in the face of our truth, superior morality, or whatever? Clearly, the state allows us to engage in these actions because they are harmless or, worse, because they reinforce the popular myth of Canadian democracy.

This degeneration into the politics of the comfort zone has led to several deformations which reinforce the continuation of this cycle of self-serving protest. One such deformation is the increasing tendency for arrest and the presumed incumbent publicity to become ends unto themselves. Within this framework, the number of arrests one has amassed becomes the proof of one's revolutionary commitment and credentials. This process, particularly rampant among men, where civil disobedience becomes a form of nonviolent machismo, is appropriately described by Judy Costello:

> I believe in noncooperation and civil disobedience, but in practice I have seen men use these tools as weapons – seeing who can suffer the most, counting up jail records, feeding on the glory of being able to suffer more.[9]

Another deformation, one which serves as a cushion against breaking with comfort zone politics, is the concept that there is no enemy, that we are *all* victims (oppressed and oppressors alike), victims of a state gone out of control. This concept is undoubtedly the result of the fact that nonviolence is often a white movement response to forms of repression which do not directly affect them, whether this takes the form of support to the Innu, Azanians, the people of Wolleston Lake or Big Mountain, or the East Timorese. It has become increasingly popular to give a nod to concepts of the oneness of it all held by indigenous peoples when searching for a theoretical underpinning to the concept of no enemy. In this vein, it is perhaps instructive to look at what Rolling Thunder, a traditional native spiritual spokesperson, has to say on this subject:

> The idea I've found in some modern people that

there's no good or bad, that it's all the same, it's pure nonsense. I know what they are are trying to say, but they don't understand it. Where we're at here in life, with all our problems, there's good and there's bad, and they better know it.[10]

As long as we remain passive and ineffective in our resistance, we will, as Ward Churchill states, leave Third and Fourth World peoples in the front line of the very real and very violent struggle between imperialism and liberation while we continue to reap the benefits of a comfort zone created by their oppression. All the pious statements and the cathartic activities we engage in change nothing. Perhaps we must look ourselves squarely in the face and see ourselves as others often see us.

[If] it is true that whites want struggles without pain – and we say that it is – then it's because they don't want new life, don't really want a new order. It means they ain't really dissatisfied with the present arrangement of power and property relations.[11]

Having dealt with what I see as the operative comfort zone politics governing the current peace movement politics, I will now turn to the thought of pacifists and nonviolent activists, both historically and currently, to attempt to ascertain the degree to which pacifism absolutely precludes violence.

Allow me first to turn to the thinking of Henry David Thoreau, particularly to his work *Civil Disobedience* (originally entitled *Resistance to Civil Government*). In this work Thoreau says "The only obligation I have a right to assume is to do at any time what I think right."[12]

And later:

> In other words, when a sixth of the population of a
> nation which has undertaken to be the refuge of
> liberty are slaves, and subjected to military law, I
> think it is not too soon for honest men [*sic*] to rebel
> and revolutionize. What makes this duty all the
> more urgent is the fact that the country so over-
> run is not our own, but ours is the invading army."[13]

Thoreau would of course condone such rebellions
and revolutionizing taking a nonviolent form. But to find
another dimension, we have only to look at his text *A
Plea for Captain John Brown*, the white, antislavery fighter
who engaged in armed struggle against the government
in opposition to slavery before finally being arrested at
Harper's Ferry, during an armed raid, and subsequently
hanged for treason:

> I do not wish to kill or be killed, but I can foresee
> circumstances in which both of these things would
> be by me unavoidable. We preserve the so-called
> peace of community of deeds of petty violence every
> day. Look at the policeman's billy and handcuffs!
> Look at the jail! Look at the gallows! Look at the
> chaplain of the regiment! We are hoping only to
> live on the outskirts of this provisional arm. I think
> that for once the Sharpes rifles and the revolvers
> were employed in a righteous cause. The tools were
> in the hands of one who could use them.[14]

And finally "The question is not about the weapon

but the spirit in which you use it."[15]

It is equally instructive to look at the thought of Martin Luther King, Jr. on this question. In particular I would like to look at the CBC Massey Lectures which Dr. King gave in 1967. In a lecture entitled *Conscience and the Vietnam War*, Dr. King said, "Every man [*sic*] of humane convictions must decide on the protest that best suits [his] convictions but we must all protest."[16]

Regarding youth and social action, he said:

> But across the spectrum of attitudes towards violence that can be found among radicals is there a unifying thread? Whether they read Gandhi or Frantz Fanon, all radicals understand the need for action – direct, self-transforming and structure-transforming action. This may be their most creative, collective insight.[17]

Finally, Dr. King's position becomes unequivocally clear in the following quote from his lectures, *Conscience and Social Change*, concerning the riots of 1967:

> This bloodlust interpretation ignores the most striking features of the city riots. Violent they certainly were. But the violence, to a startling degree, was focused against property rather than people. There were very few cases of injury to persons, and the vast majority of the rioters were not involved at all in attacking people. . . . From the facts, an unmistakable pattern emerges: a handful of Negroes used gunfire substantially to intimidate, not to kill; and all of the other participants had a different target –

property. . . . I am aware that there are many who wince at the distinction between property and persons, who hold both sacrosanct. My views are not so rigid. A life is sacred. Property is intended to serve life, and no matter how much we surround it with rights and respect, it has no personal being. It is part of the earth man [*sic*] walks on; it is not [human].[18]

I present these rather lengthy quotes because I think it is important that when we draw upon historical figures to support our strategy we recognize that their definitions of violence and nonviolence, of the line between nonviolent and violent resistance, were much less rigid than those we are now in the habit of employing. However, we need not look so far back in history or outside the current white peace movement to find evidence of a recognition that nonviolence does not imply the absolute, constant, and permanent absence of force or violence. I could offer quotes *ad nauseum* to this effect, but I will restrict myself to the following two. First, Doug Man, in an article entitled "The Movement":

One does not become nonviolent by failing to act (or acting too weakly) to prevent the prior violence; one shares responsibility for it. There are only varying degrees of violence in real situations, and the correct revolutionary action will always be the least violent one appropriate to a given set of circumstances.[19]

Second, Pat James, in an article entitled "Physical

Resistance to Attack: The Pacifist's Dilemma, the Feminist's Hope":

> Common sense as well as nonviolent principle dictate that an aggressive physical response to a threat is the last choice for self-defense. Any physical response by the victim is likely to be perceived as violence by the attacker, and the defender should use the least amount of force necessary to stop the attack.[20]

Were we to accept the level of violence defined/accepted as within the bounds of nonviolence by Man and James, then I believe we would find that the ideological distance between so-called nonviolent resisters and supporters of violent resistance in Canada today would be one of differences in analysis and chosen tactics at this point in history, rather than the absolute moral and strategic abyss we often present it as. I don't believe there is anyone on any side of the debate proposing more than appropriate violence, more than necessary force. It is simply a matter of determining, at this historical juncture, what is necessary and appropriate to stem the flood of violence of modern society, recognizing as we do the ease with which we, as a privileged social group, can fall back into the comfort zone available to us in this society as a result of this ongoing violence. If we do not proceed honestly and critically, we risk creating a situation where the adherence to nonviolence takes precedence over achieving the goals which we set for ourselves.

Nonviolence and the Third World

"National liberation, national renaissance, the restoration of nationhood to the people, commonwealth; whatever may be the formulas introduced, decolonization is always a violent phenomenon."[21]

This quote from Frantz Fanon poses a hard reality. There has never been an example of nonviolent liberation in the Third World. The one experiment with nonviolent decolonization was the electoral victory of Salvador Allende in Chile, and this one example was smashed by U.S. imperialism with such ease and brutality as to virtually eliminate the last vestiges of any illusion that Western imperialism will allow nonviolent decolonization. One has only to look to Nicaragua to see the absolute necessity for the developed capacity for violent response in a nation that frees itself from the imperialist bloc.

Again, one need only look to the African National Congress (ANC) and the example of Nelson Mandela to see why Third World revolutionaries must embrace violence. The ANC did not turn to armed struggle until June 1961, following more than a decade of nonviolent resistance. In 1952, 8,500 ANC supporters were arrested for civil disobedience actions against the pass laws, and, as a result, Mandela, among others, was banned. For continuing nonviolent resistance, Mandela was arrested and charged with treason in 1956, not to be acquitted until 1961. The prosecutor in this trial said, "If any serious threat to white rule were to arise, the shooting of 5,000 natives by machine gun would provide quiet for a long time."[22]

This model was applied against peaceful demonstrators in Sharpesville on March 21, leaving 67 dead. On May 31, 1961, a three-day peaceful strike was broken up by massive police and military intervention. Finally, pushed to the limit, the ANC turned to armed struggle, founding its military wing *Umkhoto We Sizwe* (Spear of the Nation) on June 26, 1961, and beginning a campaign of sabotage in December of the same year. Mandela, as a leading figure in *Umkhoto We Sizwe*, was arrested in August of 1962. In his 1963 trial on sedition charges, for which he languished in jail for years. Mandela explained the decision to turn to violence as follows:

> "Government violence can only do one thing and that is breed counter-violence. We have warned repeatedly that the government, by resorting continually to violence, will breed counter-violence amongst the people, until ultimately, if there is no dawning of sanity on the part of the government, the dispute will finish by being settled in violence and by force."[23]

Our responsibility goes beyond recognizing why colonized peoples are forced to turn to violence, beyond recognizing the right of colonized peoples to use violent forms of struggle. We must also recognize that there is a dialectical relationship between Third World liberation and international struggles of all other types, that the

speed and effectiveness of decolonization in the Third
World is in part determined by the effectiveness of our
resistance in the asshole of the beast. Our solidarity lies,
as George Lakey of the Movement for a New Society has
said, in actively working to bring an end to colonialism
and imperialism by attacking its centres of power.[24] We
must make such resistance central and as complete as
possible. This resistance, if it is to be effective, obliges us
to absorb some of the violence of the international confrontation. If we fail to do so, we fail to meet our responsibility to play a full and equal role in the international
revolution. We will be guilty of what Marcel Peju has
called "the wish to build up a luxury socialism upon the
fruits of imperialist robbery."[25] We will fail to meet the
challenge of Third World peoples, defined by Fanon as
follows:

> "The Third World does not mean to organize a
> great crusade of hunger against the whole of Eu-
> rope. What it expects from those who for centuries
> have kept it in slavery is that they will help to reha-
> bilitate [human]kind, and help make [humanity]
> victorious everywhere, once and for all. But it is
> clear that we are not so naive as to think this will
> come about with the cooperation of European gov-
> ernments. This huge task which consists of reintro-
> ducing [humanity] into the world, the whole of
> [human]kind, will be carried out with the indis-
> pensable help of the European people, who must
> themselves realize that in the past they have often
> joined the ranks of our common masters where

colonial questions were concerned. To achieve this the European peoples must first decide to wake up and shake themselves, use their brains, and stop playing the stupid game of Sleeping Beauty."[26]

We should not be so vain, however, as to believe that if we do not mobilize revolutionary opposition in the centre, the international revolution will cease to exist. Rather, we will simply be choosing to remain in the comfort zone while our brothers and sisters in the Third World continue to struggle for international justice at an ever greater cost to themselves. Meanwhile, we can continue to reap the benefits of their exploitation while rhetorically posing as revolutionaries.

The Internal Colonies

When we talk about colonization of the Third World, national liberation, and so forth, we generally think about South and Central America, Africa, the Middle East, and so on. Seldom do we consider the internal Third and Fourth World colonies within North America. Here, I mean the Native nations, the New Afrikan (black) Nation, occupied Puerto Rico, and northern Mexico. I wish now to turn attention to these.

Native Nations. In an article entitled "Radioactive Colonization and the Native American," Ward Churchill and Winona LaDuke demonstrate that native nations exist within both Canada and the United States. These nations, which are victims of neocolonialism, today hold a landbase which is about three percent of their original. However, the Diné (Navajo) Nation alone has a landbase equivalent in size to Luxemburg, Lichtenstein, and Monaco combined, or approximately as large as Belgium, The Netherlands, or Denmark. Further, the Diné Nation alone is richer in natural resources than all six of the above-mentioned European nations combined. By these measures, indigenous North American people should, by every standard, be among the wealthiest and healthiest of populations. Instead, by both U.S. and Canadian governmental accounts, they are the very poorest strata of society, experiencing far and away the shortest life expectancies and highest rates of infant mortality, least education, most unemployment, and greatest rates of death by malnutrition, suicide, and exposure. Churchill and LaDuke hold that all this is the direct byproduct of the internal colonization of American Indians, and that the situation must be changed.[27]

They further argue a radical native response – one which they believe is to be found in the program of the American Indian Movement, AIM – is in a position to cripple North American imperialism. This is so because the radical native position (which Churchill has elsewhere termed indigenism) is anti-imperialist both internally and externally. American Indian peoples are in a position to destroy much of the North American imperialist base by challenging its Indian policy and dismembering its domestic territorality. They can equally cripple U.S. imperialism in its external projection by depriving it of, or at least curtailing its access to, crucial resources such as uranium (about 60 percent of the North American reserves are located within Native American lands), and a range of other critical minerals as well. The implications to U.S. armaments production, for example, are obvious.[28]

This will not, however, be a peaceful struggle, and we, as Euroamerican radicals inside the North American settler states, must develop a clear position regarding what we will do if this war of genocide which has been going on for some 500 years once again heats up and heads toward a definitive culmination.

New Afrika. The struggle of New Afrikan people for independence is often regarded by the white movement as being almost archetypically violent. A particularly good example of this can be found in the Spring 1987 issue of *Kick It Over* when Malcolm X (El Hajj Malik El Shabazz) is described in a footnote as having been a competitor to Martin Luther King, presumably on the basis of Malcolm's belief that the decolonization of black people in America would be a process involving violence.[29] Whites often elect to portray these two men as ideological competitors, a matter reflecting the splits in consciousness of our own movement rather than theirs. In actuality, both Malcolm X and Martin Luther King shared a single long term goal – the liberation of black people in America. They could each be found at the same mass actions, and they both ultimately died at the hands of assassins as a result of their lifelong struggles.

We have already looked at what Dr. King had to

say regarding violence. A similar look at what Malcolm X had to say on violence reveals that, while there are differences in outlook between the two men, these are not so great as we have been led to believe. In a 1964 speech, Malcolm X said, "Now, I'm not criticizing those here who are nonviolent. I think everyone should do it the way they feel it is best, and I congratulate anyone who can remain nonviolent in the face of all [that confronts us]."[30] In a 1965 interview he goes on:

"I don't favor violence. If we could bring about recognition and respect for our people by peaceful means, well and good. Everybody would like to reach [our] objectives peacefully. But I am also a realist. The only people in this country who are asked to be nonviolent are [the oppressed]. I've never heard anyone go to the Ku Klux Klan and teach them nonviolence, or the [John] Birch Society, or other right-wing elements. Nonviolence is only preached to black Americans and I don't go along with anyone who wants to teach our people nonviolence until someone at the same time is teaching our enemy to be nonviolent. I believe we should protect ourselves by any means necessary when we are attacked by racists."[31]

This position is not unique among supposedly violence-prone black movements. For instance, Point 10 of the *Program of the Black Panther Party* reads:

"We want land, bread, housing, education, clothing, justice, and peace. And our major political ob-

jective: a United Nations-supervised plebiscite to
be held throughout the black colony in which only
black colonial subjects will be allowed to participate, for the purpose of determining the will of
black people as to their national identity."[32]

And lest one think the Panthers' policy of armed
self-defense was particularly violent and aggressive, the
following quote from party chairman Bobby Seale's "1969
Instructions to all Members" is informative:

"[N]o Panther can break the gun law unless his life
is in danger and the Party recognizes this. If he [*sic*]
does, we will expel or suspend him [*sic*] depending
on the seriousness of the offense. Panther Party
training in this area of self-defense includes a study
of gun laws, [and] safe use of weapons, and there is
a strict rule that no Party member can use a weapon
except in the case of an attack on his [*sic*] life –
whether the attacker is a police officer or any other
person. In the case of police harassment the Party
will merely print the offending officers picture in
the newspaper so the officer can be identified as an
enemy of the people . . . no attempt on his [*sic*] life
will be made."[33]

More contemporaneously, Omali Yeshitela, head
of the African People's Socialist Party, has said:

"[T]he question of peace also demands that we use
every means within our power to arm the African
masses against the attacks against our people
throughout the U.S. The question of peace must
embrace the idea of the self-reliance by the colo-

nized masses to provide their own resistance to terror, their own peace."[34]

The theme is clearly repetitive. Wherever we look among the pronouncements of New Afrikans, it is the same: land, *peace*, and self-defense. From the very origin of slavery, through the COINTELPRO repression – which saw black groups of the '60s and '70s disrupted, and black leaders imprisoned or liquidated – black people have been the victims of orchestrated genocide. Should we doubt this, we have only to recall the bombing of the MOVE house, in Philadelphia on May 13, 1985, and the subsequent blanket exoneration (in May 1988) of all the officials responsible for the mass murder which ensued. It is equally important that we never forget the final announcement of government agents before dropping their bomb: "Attention MOVE! This is America!"

Is it any surprise, given such a history, that nonviolent black organizations, such as the Congress for Racial Equality (CORE) and the Student Nonviolent Coordinating Committee (SNCC), ultimately broke with the constraints of nonviolence? As in the case of American Indians, the struggle of black people demands our concrete support. Black Panther Minister of Defense Huey P. Newton once stated it this way:

> "[W]hen we're attacked and ambushed in the Black Colony, then the white revolutionary students and intellectuals and all other whites who support the Colony should respond by attacking the enemy in *their* community."[35]

In 1969, Students for a Democratic Society (SDS), one of the main organizations of the North American anti-imperialist movement at that time, recognized the key role of black nationalism in the common struggles against capitalism and imperialism. SDS further noted that "revolutionary nationalism [is] the main factor which ties all the oppressed nations together in their fight against imperialism, and that anything less than complete support on the part of the white left would be a copout on the solidarity which we must give the worldwide movement of the oppressed peoples for liberation."[36]

Puerto Rico

The direct colonization of an island off its coast by the United States, and the exploitation of this island for military purposes and as a source of cheap labour and raw materials, has led to the rise of a national liberation struggle both on the island itself and in the United States, where many Puertorriqueños have been forced to move because of the artificially depressed economic conditions in their homeland.

Again we have at hand a nonwhite movement within North America forced to confront the question of violence in ways which are qualitatively different from that of whites. The matter need not be belabored, but I will quote from Point 12 of the Young Lords Party (formerly Young Lords Organization), a Puertorriqueño formation similar to the Panthers which was active in the

United States until the late 1970s, which states:

"WE BELIEVE ARMED SELF-DEFENSE AND
ARMED STRUGGLE ARE THE ONLY MEANS
TO LIBERATION. We are opposed to violence –
the violence of hungry children, illiterate adults,
diseased old people, and the violence of poverty
and profit. We have asked, petitioned, gone to
courts, demonstrated peacefully, and voted for poli-
ticians full of empty promises. But we still ain't free.
The time has come to defend the lives of our people against repression and for revolutionary war
against the businessman, politician, and police.
When a government oppresses our people, we have
a right to abolish it and create a new one."[37]

While the Young Lords no longer exist, other
independentista organizations have come into being
which continue the struggle both on the island of Puerto
Rico and inside the United States. Sixteen prominent
Puertorriqueño nationalists, arrested in an FBI/CIA/mili-
tary predawn raid on the island in September 1985, were
tried in Hartford, Connecticut, on charges related to the
actions of the clandestine organization los Macheteros.
As white radicals and revolutionaries supporting such
nations as Nicaragua and Third World organizations such
as the FMLN, we are duty-bound to also support this
Puertorriqueño national liberation struggle which so
closely parallels that of other Latin American anticolonial
struggles. We cannot allow ourselves to be alienated from
it because one of its fronts, which by its very nature re-

quires reliance upon armed actions, lies squarely in the heart of our North American safety zone.

Mexico

Closely related to the Puertorriqueño independentista movement is that for liberation of the northern half of Mexico, the portion north of the Rio Grande expropriated by the United States under the provisions of the 1848 Treaty of Guadalupe Hidalgo. Although the roots of this liberation struggle extend back through history all the way to the U.S. war of conquest which resulted in the treaty, its more recent manifestations began in the mid-1960s with the emergence of Reies Lopez Tijerina's Alianza Federal de Mercedes in New Mexico, Rudolfo "Corky" Gonzalez' Crusade for Justice in Colorado, and the Brown Berets in California. These were consolidated in the form of the Movimiento Liberacion Nacional Mexico (Movement for the National Liberation of Mexico, MLNM), an organization aligned with the Puertorriqueño Fuerzas Armadas de Liberacion (Armed Forces of the National Liberation, FALN). The requirements for anti-imperialist support to this Mexicano independentista movement are essentially the same as with regard to the Puertorriqueño movement (or, for that matter, with regard to Native American and New Afrikan liberation struggles).

Women and Nonviolence

Finally, I would like to look briefly at nonviolence as it applies to women, beginning with two quotes. First:

> As women, nonviolence must begin for us in the refusal to be violated, in the refusal to be victimized. We must find alternatives to submission because our submission – to rape, to assault, to domestic servitude, to abuse and victimization of every sort – perpetuates violence.[38]

And second:

> The main reason for choosing physical resistance to physical attack is that it is most likely to work . . . researchers report that the more quickly a woman responds with physical force, the less likely she will be raped, and that early recognition of danger is the single most important factor in preventing or deflecting attack.[39]

When we look at the issue of nonviolent resistance to aggression, we must consider the fact that we are dealing with many separate experiences. One of the most universal divisions must be violence as it is experienced by women under patriarchy, and violence as it is experienced by men under patriarchy. Clearly, we recognize the right of women to respond to physical and/or psychological aggression using whatever means are necessary, up to and including armed or violent self-defense or retaliation.

Nonviolence: Some Logical Inconsistencies

We accept the necessity of armed struggle in the Third World because the level of oppression leaves people with no other reasonable option. We recognize that the actions of Third World revolutionaries are not aggressive acts of violence, but a last line of defense and the only option for liberation in a situation of totally violent oppression. Similarly, an examination of the realities confronting American Indians, New Afrikans, Puertorriqueños, and Mexicanos/Chicanos, should, I believe, bring us face to face with the fact that the same sorts of Third and Fourth World circumstances and dynamics exist within the contemporary borders of the United States and Canada. Certain sectors of the peace movement have already begun to recognize this in a rudimentary kind of way. For example, the following quote comes from an open letter to the peace movement as a whole, by the advisory board of the United Methodist Voluntary Service:

> If real peace is to be achieved, the white peace movement must aggressively seek leadership and direction from blacks, Hispanics, Native Americans, and other people of colour. They must participate in all aspects of organizational planning, decision-making, and outreach. It is only with this active involvement that it will be possible to build a truly broadbased, multiracial, multicultural movement capable of winning.[40]

I would only add that we must also recognize that the reason such a movement can win is because it has the capacity to meet the violence of the state with a counterviolence of sufficient strength to dismember the heartland of the empire, liberating the oppressed nations within it. Further, we must acknowledge the absolute right of women to respond to the violence of patriarchy with the force necessary to protect themselves. In sum, we must recognize the validity of violence as a necessary step in self-defense and toward liberation when the violence of the system leaves the victim(s) with no other viable option. And it is here the logical inconsistency lies.

We recognize the right of oppressed peoples to respond to their oppression with violence, but we abstain from engaging in violence ourselves. Thus we recognize our own participation in the oppression of other peoples while we also attempt to deny the critical situation in which we ourselves are found today, a circumstance described by Rosalie Bertell in an earlier quote. If, as Bertell suggests, we are sitting upon a dying earth, and consequently dying as a species solely as a result of the nature of our society, if the technology we have developed is indeed depleting the earth, destroying the air and water, wiping out entire species daily, and steadily weakening us to the point of extinction, if phenomena such as Chernobyl are not aberrations, but are (as I insist they are) mere reflections of our daily reality projected at a level where we can at last recognize its true meaning, then is it not time – long past time – when we should do anything, indeed everything, necessary to put an end to such madness? Is it not in fact an act of unadulterated self-defense to do so?

Our adamant refusal to look reality in its face, to step outside our white skin privilege long enough to see that it is killing us, not only tangibly reinforces the oppression of people of colour the world over, it may well be the single most important contributor to an incipient omnicide, the death of all life as we know it. In this sense, it may well be that our self-imposed inability to act decisively, far from having anything at all to do with the reduction of violence, is instead perpetuating the greatest process of violence in history. It might well be that our moral position is the most mammoth case of moral bankruptcy of all time.

What Is to Be Done?

It is not my purpose here, as I understand it was not Ward Churchill's before me, to suggest that the peace movements in either the United States or Canada adopt a program of armed struggle. Rather, it is my intent, as I assume it was his, to strongly point out that the current strategies of both movements are not revolutionary, and can therefore not be expected to lead in positive, or even acceptable, directions for social change. These strategies are nothing but a complex, psychological self-deception that allows us to pose as revolutionaries from within our comfort zones. Churchill's thesis and his analysis are, in my view, 100 percent accurate.

I also find in Churchill's essay the starting point for the process which can reverse the slide into the oblivion of irrelevance, or worse, upon which we presently appear to have embarked. I quote a passage which must be considered key in this regard:

> What is at issue . . . is not the replacement of hegemonic pacifism with some cult of terror. Instead, it is the realization that in order to be effective and ultimately successful, any revolutionary movement within advanced capitalist nations must develop the broadest possible range of thinking/action by which to confront the state. This should be conceived not as an array of component forms of struggle, but as a continuum of activity stretching from petitions/letter writing and so forth through mass mobilizations/demonstrations, onward into the arena of armed self-defense, and still onward through the realm of offensive military operations (e.g., elimination of critical state facilities, targeting of key individuals within the coporate apparatus, etc.). All this must be apprehended as a holism, as an internally consistent liberatory process applicable at this generally formulated level to the late capitalist context no less than to the Third World. From the basis of this fundamental understanding and, it may be asserted, only from this basis can a viable liberatory praxis for [North America] emerge.[41]

I am arguing that on the basis of the recognition of

the interrelatedness implied in such a continuum, in such a spectrum of activity, we begin to seriously recognize our current shortcomings for what they are: dogma which must be replaced by honest theory, a reactionary rote-like protest which has displaced honest practice. I am arguing that we recognize, as Barbara Deming has, that:

> There is a sense even in which we do share the same faith. When we define the kind of world we want to bring into being, our vision and theirs too is of a world in which no person exploits another, abuses, dominates another – in short, a nonviolent world. We differ about how to bring this world into being: and that's a very real difference. But we are in the same struggle and we need each other. We need to take strength from each other, and we need to learn from each other. . . . I think it is very important that we not be too sure that they have all the learning to do, and we have all the teaching. It seems obvious to us right now that the methods they are sometimes willing to use are inconsistent with the vision we both hold of the new world. It is just possible – as we pursue that vision – that we are in some way inconsistent, too, for we have been in the past.[42]

I am suggesting that we must recognize a symbiosis between our struggles, that when any of us are stronger, all of us are stronger; when any of us are weaker, all of us are weaker. I am suggesting that we develop a genuine praxis, and here I am using praxis, as Churchill did, to mean action consciously and intentionally guided by theory while simultaneously guiding the evolution of theoretical elaboration.[43] If we fail to do so, we abdicate our revolutionary responsibility and remain for the oppressed of this earth nothing more than Her Majesty's Loyal Opposition.

Notes

1. Ward Churchill,and Mike Ryan, *Pacifism as Pathology* (Winnipeg: Arbeiter Ring, 1998).

2. Kelly Booth, "Nonviolence: The Way of Nature," *New Catalyst*, Vol. I, No. 3 (Mar./Apr. 1986), p. 3.

3. *Ibid.*

4. Rosalie Bertell, "Early War Crimes of World War III," in *A Case for NonViolent Resistance* (Toronto: Cruise Missile Conversion Project, 1984), p. 23.

5. Anonymous, "Thoughts on Consolidation," *Notes From a New Afrikan POW Journal*, Vol. 7, p. 35.

6. Anonymous, "Nonviolent Solidarity with a Violent Struggle," *Pornography, Rape, War: Making the Links,* Women's Action for Peace/Alliance for NonViolent Action, pamphlet (Fall 1984), p. 33.

7. *Ibid.*

8. Churchill, op. cit., p.49.

9. Judy Costello, "Beyond Gandhi: An American Feminists Approach to Nonviolence," in *Reweaving the Web of Life*, Pam McAllister, ed. (Philadelphia: New Society, 1982), pp. 179-80.

10. Rolling Thunder, cited in *The Vancouver Five: A Story of Struggle to Protect the Earth*, anonymous, undated, no page numbers.

11. Shanna Bakari, "On Concrete Solidarity," *Notes From a New Afrikan POW Journal*, Vol. 2, p. 33.

12. Henry David Thoreau, *Civil Disobedience*, photocopy pamphlet, p. 236.

13. *Ibid.*

14. Henry David Thoreau, "A Plea for Captain John Brown," in *John Brown* (Montreal: privately published, 1984), p. 22.

15. *Ibid.*

16 Martin Luther King, "Conscience and the Vietnam War," in *Conscience and Social Change* (Toronto: CBC Productions, The Massey Lectures), 1967, p. 18.

17. Martin Luther King, "Youth and Social Action," in *Ibid.*, p. 23.

18. Martin Luther King, "Conscience and the Vietnam War," op. cit., p. 32.

19. Doug Man, "The Movement," *New Catalyst*, Vol. 1, No. 8 (Mar./Apr., 1986), p. 17.

20. Pat James, "Physical Resistance to Attack: The Pacifist's Dilemma, The Feminists Hope," in *Reweaving the Web of Life*, Pam McAllister, ed., op. cit., p. 389.

21. Frantz Fanon, *The Wretched of the Earth* (New York: Evergreen Black Cat Edition, 1968), p. 35.

22. Nelson Mandela, *It Is Our Duty to Resist* (Hartford, Connecticut: Worldview Forum, 1986), p. 6.

23. *Ibid.*, p. 22.

24. George Lakey, *A Manifesto for Nonviolent Revolution* (WIN) , p. 25.

25. Marcel Peju, cited in Frantz Fanon, op. cit., p. 103.

26. Frantz Fanon, op. cit., p. 106.

27. Ward Churchill and Winona LaDuke, "Radioactive Colonization and the Native American," *Socialist Review*, No. 81 (Spring 1986), p. 77.

28. *Ibid.*, p. 118. For Churchill's use of the terms indigenist and indigenism, *see* his "On Support of the Indian Resistance in Nicaragua: A Statement of Position and Principle," *Akwesasne Notes*, Vol. 18, No. 5 (Autumn 1986).

29. *Kick It Over*, "Anarchafilmmaker: An Interview with Lizzie Borden," No. 18 (Spring 1987), p. 3 (from a footnote on this page).

30. Malcolm X, *Malcolm X Talks to Young People* (New York: Pathfinder, 1965), p. 4.

31. *Ibid.*, p. 15.

32. Philip S. Foner, ed., *The Black Panthers Speak* (Philadelphia/ New York: J. B. Lippencott, 1970), p. 3.

33. *Ibid.*, p. 85.

34. Omali Yeshitela, *The Struggle for BREAD, PEACE, and BLACK POWER* (Oakland, California: Burning Spear, 1981), p. 65.

35. Philip S. Foner, op. cit., p. 55.

36. *Ibid.*, p. 229.

37. *Ibid.*, p. 237.

38. Anonymous, *Redefining Violence*, a pamphlet, no place or publisher (5 April, 1975), p. 72.

39. Pat James in *Reweaving the Web of Life*, Pam McAllister, ed., op. cit., p. 389.

40. Anonymous, *Women's Encampment for a Future of Peace and*

Justice: Resource Handbook, Seneca Army Depot Peace Camp (Summer 1983), p. 23.

41. Churchill, op. cit., pp.91–92.

42. Barbara Demming, *On Anger*, pamphlet reprinted from *Liberation* (Palo Alto, California: Institute for the Study of Nonviolence), no date, p. 2.

43. Churchill, op.cit., p.84.

Index

A

B

"The question is not *whether* to use

violence in the global class struggle

to end the rule of international

imperialism, but only *when* to use it."

Pacifism, the ideology of nonviolent political action, has become all but universa
among the more progressive elements of contemporary mainstream North America
In Pacifism as Pathology, scholar-activist Ward Churchill dares to ask som
uncomfortable questions about that ideology

He argues that while pacifism promises that the harsh
realities of state power can be transcended through good
feelings and purity of purpose, it is in many ways a
counter-revolutionary movement that defends and reinforce
the same status-quo it claims to oppose. Mike Ryan
responds to Churchill's essay, further developing it in
consideration of a Canadian context

Pacifism as Pathology is an important intervention into the delusion, aroma o
racism, and sense of privilege which mark the covert self-defeatism of mainstream
dissident politics. It is written in the hope that others — many others — will begin
to seriously address the issue

Printed in Canada

ISBN 1-894037-07-3

PACIFISM AS PATHOLOGY RE $9.95

1-894037-07-3 CHURCHILL WARD   NEW 08
NEW-POWE 01 POLIT-ACTIV/PEAC728

U
Politics / Ideas

ARBEITER RI
publishi